Asako Takami
Memories of India and Odissi Dance

インド回想記
オディッシーダンサー 高見麻子

高見麻子 著 *Asako Takami*
田中晴子 編 *Haruko Tanaka*

Asako Takami (April 19, 1960 - November 3, 2007).　　Photographed by Ryosen Kono

どうか

捧げてください

動きひとつひとつを

一番美しい

一番力に満ちた

あなた自身に

そして輝きなさい

身体は賢いです

信頼をこめて

波長を合わせてください

みなさんはこのことをもう知ってるってわかっています

だけど

ただなにかを送りたかったのです 踊りのために

みなさんのことを想っています

私もとりくんでいることです

（2006年5月24日、舞台の前に生徒たちへの言葉）

for your performance on may 26th

please

offer

every movement

to

your most beautiful,

most powerful,

you.

and shine.

our body is wise

tune into it

with trust

i know you know all this

but

i just wanted to send you something for your dancing.

i'm thinking of you

i am also working on it.

(May 24, 2006, her words for the students.)

インド回想記　オディッシーダンサー 高見麻子

クムクムさんのクムクム	9
夜明けのチャイ	23
クムクムさんのお花	31
クムクムさんのサリーのこと	35
オールドデリーで	41
クムクムさんが日本にいた83年から87年までのこと	45
ひと針ひと針	57
オディッシー	67
インド	75
ケルチャラン モハパトラ グルジーの東京ワークショップ	83
ブバネシュワールへのバスの旅	95
ケルチャラン グルジー	99
ブバネシュワール ミシュラ ジー	107
河むこうの トリナート マハラナ ジー	115
康 米那さん	121
サンジュクタさんの最期	137
グル	147
あとがき	159
麻子とコンテンポラリーダンス　　文・ラルフ レモン	165
From her journal 日記より	173
謝辞	176
略歴	178
日本での主な活動	182
あとがきのあとがき　　文・田中晴子	187

Asako Takami
Memories of India and Odissi Dance

Kumkum ji's kumkum	14
Chai at Dawn	26
Kumkum ji's Flowers	32
About Kumkum ji's Sarees.	37
In Old Delhi	42
Japan	50
Hito hari hito hari (One stitch at a time)	61
Odissi	70
India	78
Kelucharan Mohapatra Guruji's Tokyo Workshop	88
The Bus Trip to Bhubaneswar.	96
Kelucharan Guruji	102
Bhubaneswar Mishra ji	110
Trinath Maharana ji across the river	118
Mina Kang	128
Sanjukta Panigrahi	141
Guru	153
Afterword	161
Asako and contemporary dance _Ralph Lemon_	168
From her journal	173
Acknowledgments	177
Profile	180
Works in Japan	184
Afterword of afterword _Haruko Tanaka_	193

クムクムさんのクムクム

　チリンチリンという金の腕輪の音とともに、ナハー（沐浴、シャワー）のあと、クムクムさんが、ほどよく糊のきいた木綿のサリーを身にまとう。朝のいい匂いの空気の中、鳥のさえずりの響く中、ひんやりと薄暗いベッドルームの隅で。

　クムクムさんの眉間のところはほのかに赤く染まっている。掌にオイルを一滴たらして赤い粉をペースト状にする。それを右手の薬指と小指で、今日のビンディーを描いてゆく。まず真ん中に小さな点を小指でおいて、とんとんとちょっぴりずつその点を大きくしていってちょうどよい大きさにする。最後の仕上げに（ここが私が大好きなところ）、赤い粉をビンディーにまぶすようにのせると、何度見ても、うわーっきれいと思わず口から洩れてしまうような美しさになる。見とれている私を横目でみて、クムクムさんは ふふん と笑いながら、その赤いビンディーの下にカジャール（アイライナー）で小さなドットをつける。その一連の行為はそのあとに始まる朝のプージャ（供養）の一環のように神聖に感じられた。

クムクムさんの涼しげな額に赤い朝日が昇って一日は始まる。

　クムクムさんの名前「クムクム」は額に付ける赤い粉のこと。元来、クムクムの粉はアージュナーチャクラを刺激するため、何種類かのハーブ（ウコンなど）をすりあわせて混ぜ合わせたものだという。

　私もサリーを着る時は儀式のような気持ちでお寺からいただいてきたクムクムの粉を、クムクムさんと同じようにつけていた。最後の粉の加減は難しく、時々付けすぎると鼻の頭に粉が散って赤鼻になってしまっていた。でもとにかくそんなことで、ワッペンのように貼る、糊付きシールの、あの主流（？）のビンディーは、どうしてもピンとこなくて、付ける気がしない。

　クムクムさんのサリーはいつもすごく素敵だった。思わずほめると、
　「私の母のサリーです」
　とおっしゃった。毎日、今日はどんな装いなんだろうといつもとても楽しみだった。

　その頃の生活はこんな感じだ。まずナハーして身支度を整え、朝のチャ

イをいただく。ナハーとは「沐浴」という意味で、街角の井戸から汲んだ水で身を清めるという意味合いだ。カルカッタの街角で、人々が井戸のそばで身体を洗っているのをよく見た、これが私のナハーのもともとのイメージ。でもクムクムさんのお宅では普通にシャワーを浴びていた。シャワーというよりはナハーというのがいい。クムクムさんがプージャをしている間に、内弟子の私と手伝いのネパール人の男性が掃除をすませる。プージャは、日本のお家で神棚や仏壇にその日のご飯と水を挙げ、鐘を叩いて手を合わせたり、柏手を打ったりするように、祭壇に供養す

ることだ。独特の線香（ドゥーパ）のとてもいい香りが好きだった。そして朝食の支度だ。クムクムさんの家でたくさんのインド家庭料理を教わった。

　食事はだいたい家で朝、昼、晩作って食べていた。たまに
　「インド料理以外のものが食べたいですか？」
　と聞いてくれ、中心街へ中華料理やピザを食べに連れて行ってくれた。

　それでも、ときどきこっそり街の屋台で食べた。クムクムさんからは不衛生で悪い油を使っているし、病気になったら大変だから屋台で食べないようにと言われていたけど、私は屋台でたっぷり食べていた。ジェレビー、チャナプリ、サモサ、なんでもかたっぱしから食べてみた。まあ、たいてい油で揚げてあって辛くて、というのと甘ーいのとの組み合わせ。

　午前中は踊りを教えてもらう。

　午後は午睡と、静かにその日教えてもらったことを復習したりして過ごした。

ベッドルームがふたつの小さなアパートメントだった。メインベッド
ルームをクムクムさん夫妻が使い、もうひとつのベッドルームは私が使
わせてもらっていた。手伝いの人はリビングルームのソファで寝ていた。
クムクムさんはよく芸術家を招き、自分の家に泊まってもらってデリー
での活躍をささえていた。お客さんが来ると、私がベッドルームをお客
さんに譲り、リビングのソファで眠り、手伝いの人はバルコニーのソファ
で眠ることになった。

　親しくなっても聞いていいのかわからないことだったが、クムクムさ
んのご主人は「書記官」というカースト（インドの身分制度）だと話し
てくれた。クムクムさんのカーストがご主人のカーストより少し上とさ
れているもので、妻が結婚相手より少し上のカーストという組み合わせ
はインドではよくあることだそうだ。

　日常会話のヒンディー語はクムクムさんから教えてもらった。東京か
らインドに帰ることになったクムクムさんのあとを追うように、私はイ
ンドに渡った。引っ越してすぐはむりだから、最初にオリッサに行きな
さいと言われ、87年、その年に開校したオディッシーリサーチセンター
で練習というより、鍛冶屋さんで鍛えるように踊りをしてから、デリー
のクムクムさんの家に内弟子として滞在した。

Kumkum ji's kumkum

The tinkling sound of gold bangles could be heard coming from the corner of the cool, dimly lit bedroom, as Kumkum ji got ready after bathing. She wore a cotton saree, of finely spun cotton. There was a nice scent of the morning present and there was an echo of the birds singing.

Kumkum ji prepared the kumkum which is the red dye that she adorned her forehead with. She poured a drop of oil in her palm and made a paste with the red powder. She drew the day's bindi with her ring finger and little finger. First, she placed a small point in the middle with her little finger, gradually increasing the point slightly and making it a good size. For the finishing touch, which I loved, she dusted the red powder over the bindi. Oh, how exquisite! It always took my breath away, regardless of how many times I saw it. With a sidelong glance, Kumkum ji, would smile at me. Finally, she put a small dot with kajal, under that red bindi. This series of actions

Photographed by Bob Giles

felt sacred somehow, much like the morning puja that would follow shortly afterward.

A red morning sun arose with the freshly adorned forehead of Kumkum ji and the day had begun.

The word kumkum in "Kumkum ji" 's name means this red powder that adorns the forehead. It is a mixture of some herbs including turmeric mixed together to stimulate the Ajna chakra. This is considered to be the "third eye" according to Hindu tradition, a part of the brain that can be made more powerful through meditation and yoga.

Whenever I get dressed up in a saree, I like to wear the red kumkum powder that I got from the temple, performing the ritual, just like Kumkum ji. Adding and removing the excess powder at the end is difficult, and sometimes I get scattered powder on my nose which turns my nose red. But the kumkum paste done this way feels traditional and authentic, unlike the modern "sticker bindis".

Kumkum ji's sarees were always very nice. Whenever I complimented her on them, she would reply,

"these are my mother's sarees".

Every day, I looked forward to seeing the style and type of saree she would wear.

Life in those days in Delhi involved roughly the same routine every day. I would start the day with nahana; get dressed; and then have morning chai. Nahana means "bathing".

I thought back to the time I had traveled to KoIkata and I remembered seeing people, gathered around a well. They washed their bodies by the side of the well. This was my initial image of the word "nahana". At Kumkum ji's house, we took a shower in the conventional way. However, I didn't like to use the word, shower. It felt better referring to it as nahana.

At that time, I was a dance student and I stayed with Kumkum ji. While Kumkum ji was doing puja, I would help clean up, together with a Nepalese boy who did the housework. Puja is worship to God at an altar just as in a Japanese house. People bring the rice and water of the day to the shrine just as in the Buddhist altar. They ring a bell or put their hands together to pray or clap hands to Kashiwade. I liked the very unique scent of incense or "dhoop" that was used in pujas.

After the puja came preparation for breakfast. I learned a lot of Indian home cooking at Kumkum ji's house. Meals were prepared in the morning, afternoon, and evening. Occasionally, Kumkum ji would ask me, kindly, "Do you want to eat something other than Indian food?"

She sometimes took me to the city center to eat Chinese food or pizza.

At other times, I secretly ate food that was sold on the street. Kumkum ji had advised me, "please don't eat any street food. It may be unhygienic and they may have used bad oil. It would be very bad if you get sick." Yet, I secretly ate plenty of street food! I tried jilebi, channa/puri and samosas. I tried a lot of different types of street foods, although on the whole, they tended to be a combination of deep fried, very spicy items or very sweet snacks.

Kumkum ji taught me Odissi dance in the morning.
Afternoon consisted of a nap and quiet time. This allowed me to be able to review what I had been taught that day.

Her home was a two bedroomed, small apartment. Kumkum ji and her husband used the main bedroom, and I used the other one. The boy who helped with household work slept on the sofa in the living room. Kumkum ji often invited artists to her home and had them stay overnight at her house. She wanted to support their artistic endeavors in Delhi. When guests came, I gave up the bedroom for the guests and slept on the sofa in the living room. The helper boy slept on the sofa in the balcony.
Kumkum ji shared information with me about her caste and her husband's caste (the caste system is an Indian social status system).

Although we became close friends, I didn't ever quite feel comfortable asking her more about this, even though I would have liked to have known more. What she had told me and what I understood was that her husband was from a caste called the "secretary caste". Kumkum ji's caste was apparently slightly above that of her husband. It seems that this arrangement where the wife's caste is slightly above the husband's, was common in India.

I had first met Kumkum ji while she was living in Tokyo. Subsequently, I followed her when she moved from Tokyo to India. Since she was not able to teach immediately after her move back to India, she encouraged me to go to the state of Orissa first (this was the land of temples and the birthplace of Odissi dance). In 1987, the Odissi Research Center had just opened in Orissa. It was a dance institute, but didn't feel much like dance practice to me. My feeling was, that training as a dancer there was analogous to a piece of iron being worked on by a blacksmith. After I had spent some time at the Odissi Research Center, I went to meet Kumkum ji in Delhi. There, I stayed at her house, as her disciple. From Kumkum ji, I also learned the Hindi language, as used in everyday conversation.

Photographed by Bob Giles

夜明けのチャイ

　インドに行くとみんなチャイ中毒になってしまう。私もかなり重度の
中毒だった。今でも朝の黄金色の光りを見ればすぐにチャイが飲みたく
なってしまう。

　クムクムさんの家で朝起きて部屋を出ると、ダイニング・テーブルの
上にお盆にのったティーのセットが待っている。冷めないように帽子を
かぶったステンレスのポット、あっためたミルクの入ったステンレス
のミルク入れ、ステンレスの砂糖入れとカップ、各々起きた人から朝の
ティーをいただく。

　たいてい、みんなが起き出す頃を見計らって家の仕事をしてくれるネ
パールの少年バードールが用意してくれるのだけれど、誰でも先に起き
た人が、まだティーがセットされていなければ、用意するようになって
いた。

　私はベランダの椅子に座り、踊りのノートをひざにおいて、目の前の

大きなユーカリの樹々がゆれるのを見ながらいつも飲んでいた。ゆったりとした一日の始まりのゆったりとした朝の時間。時々、野生の孔雀が樹にとまってたり歩いてたりする。

　起き抜けのパジャマのティー、そして身支度を終えて軽い朝食と共に、ティー、踊りの稽古の合間のチャイ、踊りの稽古のあとのチャイ、昼食、昼寝のあと日暮れ前のティー……。そして私はそれにも飽き足らずにちょっと散歩、と外に出ては道端のチャイ屋の板の椅子に座っておじさん達といっしょに小さなカップの甘いチャイをすすっていた。

　早朝３時頃、目がさえて眠れず、暗い台所で音をたてないようにチャイを作ってショールにくるまり、ベランダで座っていた。今、思い返すとそんなことがよくあったような気がする。大きな大きな星がキガキガと輝いていた。

　　　　ティー：クムクムさんとアショカさんはこれを飲む。ポットから
　　　　アッサムティを入れ、ミルクと砂糖をちょぴっと入れたさらさら
　　　　のもの
　　　　チャイ：なべにミルクと小さな玉たまの紅茶と砂糖を入れてぐつ
　　　　ぐつ煮出す。トロトロの甘いやつ。

　クムクムさんとサモサを買いに行くとき、たまに道端の階段でチャイを飲む。クムクムさんも楽しそうに嬉しそうに坐って。私は嬉しくなる。
　朝食はさらっと軽く、トーストにバター、ジャム、ときどき卵、ビスケットなんかですませてしまう時もあった。インドでは、昼はしっかりどっしり食べるけど、朝と言えばやはりティーだった。

Chai at Dawn

Everyone who goes to India, becomes addicted to chai. I also became quite considerably addicted to it. Even now, when I see the glow of the morning golden light, I know that I will soon want to drink a cup of chai.

At Kumkum ji's home, upon waking in the morning and walking out of my bedroom, I would be greeted with a tea set waiting on a tray on the dining table. This included a stainless steel tea pot wrapped in a hat to prevent it from getting cold; a stainless steel milk container with warm milk, a stainless steel sugar canister and cups. Each person who got up in the home, would have tea like this.

Usually the Nepalese boy, Badur would prepare tea as soon as everyone got up. On occasion, if anyone woke up first and the tea was not set and ready yet, they would then make the tea for the others.

I would sit on the balcony chair and drink tea with my dance notebook on my lap, watching the large eucalyptus trees in front of me. This was a relaxing morning time to start the day. Sometimes wild peacocks could be seen in the trees and walking around on the ground below.

I had tea in my pajamas in the morning. After getting dressed up, I had tea once again with a light breakfast. I had chai between dance lessons and chai after dance practice. I had tea after lunch; after a nap; and in the late afternoon before it got dark. I also had chai when I went for a little walk outside. I would sometimes sit on a wooden bench of a chai shop on the roadside and would sip a small cup of sweet chai with the chai vendor guy.

When I think back now, I remember there were times, perhaps at 3 o'clock in the morning, when I could not sleep. I would quietly get up and make myself some chai. I made chai in the dark kitchen, taking care to avoid making a sound and waking the household. I would drink it on the balcony with the big, big stars shining brightly.

When Kumkum ji and her husband, Ashok ji had tea, it was made differently from chai. For tea, they would pour assam tea from the pot, and then add a little milk and sugar.

However for chai, they would make this by putting milk, cardamom, small ball shaped tea leaves and sugar together in a pot and boil it all together. It would become sweet and thick chai.

When Kumkum ji and I went shopping for samosas, we occasionally had chai on the roadside sitting on some stairs. Kumkum ji would sit, drinking her chai, looking happy. This in turn made me happy.

Breakfast at Kumkum ji's house was mostly light. There were times when we had toast with butter and jam; sometimes it was eggs; sometimes we had biscuits. We had a solid, bigger meal at lunch, but breakfast was mainly tea.

Photographed by Bob Giles

クムクムさんのお花

　ハーラシンハの花（インド夜香木）
　プージャの時、神様に花環をつくるため、落ちた花をひろってくる。クムクムさんちのアパートの敷地内にあるハーラシンハ。小さな小花。白く、オレンジ色のかすかなラインが花の内側にある。注意深くなるべく新鮮な落ちたばかりの花を探す。そんな時は、踊りのアビナヤを練習する私。（アビナヤとは物語を語る踊りで、花を拾う動作がオディッシーの踊りにはよくある。）

　　　朝に落つ　ハーラシンハの　花かざり
　　　アマルターシュ（ナンバンサイカチ）
　　　みあげれば　やさしき　黄花　朝　風にゆれ

　ラートキラーニー（夜香木）
　ラートキラーニーはハーラシンハと比べると肉厚でプルメリアのようだけどどこか、夜の青みを帯びていているような花でクムクムさんのベッドルームの窓辺から見える。

　　　わがままな　夜の王女に　酔う　酔う

Kumkum ji's Flowers

The following are flowers I was introduced to at Kumkum ji's place:

Harsingar (night jasmine).
At the time of a puja, we made a flower garland for the gods. We collected fallen flowers on the ground. There were some harsingar plants on the premises of Kumkum ji's apartment. They were small flowers with a faint line of orange inside the white flower. Carefully I searched for fresh flowers as much as possible. While doing so, I would practice dancing my abhinaya (expressional dance). The act of collecting flowers is a part of many Odissi abhinaya dance items.

In the morning,
Harsingar falling,
Flower garlands.

Amaltas,
The yellow flower,
Swaying in the morning wind.

Raat ki Rani

The petals of the Raat ki Rani are thick compared to Harsingar. It looks like plumeria, but sometimes it looked like a bluish flower, especially at night, when I saw it from Kumkum ji's bedroom window.

> The selfish evening princess,
> By her, getting intoxicated,
> Being drunk, drunk.

クムクムさんのサリーのこと

　毎日毎日、私はクムクムさんの毎日替わるサリー姿を見るのが本当に好きだった。新しいサリーを着て部屋から出てくるクムクムさんは、毎回フレッシュで小さな美しい花のようだった。

　夏は上質のとても薄いコットンのサリー。ボーダーが細くシンプルで、白っぽいもの、白や淡いほのかなピンクや黄緑、色がついていても、ひだのよっているところ、そしてところどころにポチポチとかすかにピンクっぽいかなぁと色味がわかる程度。

　クムクムさんのミドルネームは「ユーヴラニ」（お姫さま）で、クムクムさんのお父さんが一人娘（兄と弟がいる）につけた名前だとクムクムさんはちょっと照れて笑いながら教えてくれた。私はぴったりだなぁと思ってたけど。

　サリーブラウスは、オリッサのガムチャ織でつくったものが多く、腕ぐりのところに細いボーダーの模様があった。私はもちろんまねして、

いっぱいそういうブラウスを作った。クムクムさんの腕はひじのところ
の角度が、いかにも腕をよく使う踊り手の腕だった。

　冬は絹のサリーにピッタリとしたカシミアのカーディガン。緑のサ
リーなら緑のカーディガン、赤いサリーなら赤いカーディガン。金のちっ
ちゃなボタンがついていてそれをセーターのようにぴったりと着て、パ
ルーをカーディガンの後ろの外にたらして　というスタイル。みんな新
しいもののわけではなく、ずーっと前に買ったのや、お母さんの代から
のを大切にきちんと手入れをしてきている。だからまたいっそう美しく
見えるのかな、サリーが。

About Kumkum ji's Sarees.

Every day, I really liked seeing her sarees. Kumkum ji would come out of her room wearing a new or different saree each day. She was like a fresh, small, beautiful flower every time.

Her sarees in the summer were made of very thin cotton of fine quality. Mostly the saree borders were narrow and simple. There were whitish colored sarees; white or pale, faint pink or yellowish green sarees. The colors were very subtle and seen more prominently only at the folds and pleats. The rest was a subtle pinkish hue.

Kumkum's middle name is Yuvrani meaning "princess." Kumkum ji told me shyly with a smile, that the name was given by her father to his one and only daughter (she has an older and a younger brother). I thought the name, princess, was perfectly suited to her.

There were many saree blouses made with Orissa's gamcha fabric with a thin border pattern on the arms. Of course, I copied her style and made a lot of such blouses for myself too. Kumkum ji's elbow angles and arms were slim like those of a dancer who often used her arms.

In winter, she would put on slender, cashmere cardigans with her silk sarees. With a green saree, she would wear a green cardigan. With a red saree, it was a red cardigan. The cardigans had small gold buttons and she wore them as sweaters, but would pull the pallu of the saree out over the cardigan. Her sarees were not all that new. But they were carefully and meticulously maintained. She may have bought some of them a long time ago. Or some of them may have been passed down from her mother. I wondered if her sarees looked more beautiful because of her care and the tradition.

Photographed by Ryosen Kono

オールドデリーで

　オールドデリーのパラッタの美味しい店に行きましょう　と二人でリキシャでオールドデリーへよく行った。デリーの南の端から北の端までちょっとしたデイトリップ。入り組んだ小さな路につづく店。ドゥパを買う店もあった。

In Old Delhi

"Let's go to the delicious shop selling parathas in Old Delhi", she said. Then the two of us rode on the rickshaw to Old Delhi. It was a bit of a day trip from the south end of Delhi to the northern end. A small intricate road led to the store. There, also, was the store where we used to buy dhoop, or incense.

Photographed by Bob Giles

クムクムさんが日本にいた83年から87年までのこと

　始まりは、1983年オディッシー舞踊家サンジュクタ パニグラヒさん
が来日して草月ホールでコンサートをしたことだった。サンジュクタさ
んは、グル ケルチャラン モハパトラのもっとも卓越した弟子の一人で
世界中でオディッシーを披露していた。

　クムクムさんは、1983年の春、ご主人のアショカさんの仕事の関係
で日本に来た。そして、7月ごろには Plan B という中野富士見町にあ
る小さな地下の劇場でパフォーマンスをした。そのころ、私は前年イン
ドへ初めて旅行し、そしてサンジュクタ パニグラヒさんの公演を観た
すぐあとで、まだその興奮で、自分が自分の身体から半分もどっていな
いような感覚が残っている時だった。

　パフォーマンスが終わって1階のカフェで友人と坐っていると、衣装
をサリーに着替えてまだ顔のメークアップをしたままのクムクムさんが
そばを通過。となりの友人が
　「アサコちゃん、電話番号を聞いてみたら…」

私は最初の生徒になった。

　クムクムさんは、東京大井町、旗の台のビルディング全体がはげコンクリートの大きな会議室のような家に住んでいた。インドの香とスパイスの匂い。玄関から2階へと行くと部屋には陽がさんさんとあたっていた。台所で第一回目のレッスン。3000円くらいを小さな和紙の封筒に入れてお渡しすると、
　「大丈夫ですか？　ムリしないでください。ずっと続けるのですから」
とおっしゃった。

　その後、クラスは近くの幼稚園で行われた。生徒は、2、3人くらいの自主運営だった。一応私が最初の生徒だったので、場所探し、場所とりなど事務的な仕事は私に最初にきた。クラスのあとのチャイが主に楽しみだった。
　クムクムさんは、来日してすぐ日本語を習い始めていた。黒板に
　「クンクマ」
と大きく書いた。踊りを教えているときにも、「右」とか「左」とか日本語を加えるようになった。
　クムクムさんは、自らがアーティストであり、また、アーティストを

招き厚くもてなした。ご自宅はまるでサロンのようだった。パーティを開いて、ホームパフォーマンス、コンサートの場を提供された。私たち生徒もいつもよんでくれて、台所を手伝ったりしながら楽しかった。ラジャスターン地方の絵解き芸人ボーパたちが来てボーパ絵巻を見せてくれた時は、太い歌声が家中に響き、私はラジャスターンの砂漠にいるようだった。

　クラスのあと、駅で牛乳を一気飲みして、みんなスッキリ、汗びっしょりの電車の中だった。大井町線から終点の下高井戸。下高井戸から三軒茶屋まで若林を通って、二両編成のチンチン電車だ。40分以上は終点から終点なので降りそびれる心配もなく、その日習ったことを全部ノートに書き込んで覚えた。集中して、鉄は早いうちに打て　だ。

　クムクムさん、車の上にショールを置いたまま、走っていってしまう、そんなことがあった。
　大切なのは、人とのくらべあいでなくて、自分が変容していくプロセスかもしれない。クムクムさんの踊りへの姿勢が反映するのだと思うけど、クラスはわきあいあいだった。私は一人で近くの小さな区の会議室を借りて練習した。1時間でも30分でも場所がとれたら飛んで行ってひとつの動き、例えば手首の動きだけでもくりかえしやったりした。友

だちがいっしょにやろと言えば、飛んでった。わからないから教えてと言われたら飛んでって何度でも何度でもくりかえし、彼女ができるようになるまでやった。その他のことは全く覚えていないくらい踊りざんまいだった。人は一生に一回、誰でもこんな激しい芽吹きの時を経験するのだろうけれど、まさに私は踊りで全身の細胞のひとつひとつが変化していくのを感じていた。布団に横たわり、足がじんじん じんじんするのを楽しみながら、また頭の中で今日習ったことをくまなく復習。どんな細かいことでも全部ひとこと、ひとこと、一動作、一動作目の中に思い出して記憶した。

Photographed by Bob Giles

Japan

From 1983 to 1987, Kumkum ji was in Japan.

At the beginning of that time, in 1983, Sanjukta Panigrahi, a well renowned Odissi dancer and a prominent disciple of Guru Kelucharan Mohapatra, came to Japan and performed a concert at Sogetsu Hall.

In the spring of 1983, Kumkum ji came to Tokyo, Japan, because of her husband, Ashok's work. And in July of that year, she had a performance at a small underground theater in Nakano, Fujimi cho called Plan B.

At that time, I was still feeling the excitement that I had felt after watching Sanjukta Panigrahi perform. There was a feeling that I was not yet back in my body.

After Kumkmu ji's performance, I was sitting with a friend at the cafe on the first floor. Kumkum ji had changed clothes to a saree and still had her dance make-up on, when she happened to pass by the cafe. My friend said,

"Asako chan, why don't you ask her for her contact phone number?"

Photographed by Bob Giles

And so, I became Kumkum ji's first student.

Kumkum ji, was living in Hatano-dai Oimachi in Tokyo. The whole building was like a large conference room with bald concrete. There was a scent of Indian incense and spices. When I went from the entrance to the second floor, the room was in full sunlight. The first lesson took place in the kitchen. When I handed her about 3000 yen or so as tuition, wrapped in a small washi envelope, she said,

"are you all right? Please, do not pay too much, because you are going to continue dance lessons."

After that, the class was held in the nearby kindergarten school. There were 2 or 3 students. The class was managed by us. Since I was the first student at the time, all the administrative work such as searching for and booking the venues was my responsibility. Having chai after the class was so much fun.

Kumkum ji began learning Japanese as soon as she came to Japan. On the blackboard, she wrote the word "Kunkuma" in large Japanese

Photographed by Bob Giles

letters. Even while she was teaching dance, she started to say "right" and "left" in Japanese.

Kumkum ji herself was an artist and she also invited other artists to join her and treated them with great hospitality. Her house was like a salon. She hosted parties and concerts in her home. She invited the students always to join her. We enjoyed such occasions, while helping out in the kitchen. Once we saw the Bhopas or priest singers of Rajasthan telling a story. Their thick voices echoed throughout the house. I felt as if I was in the desert of Rajasthan.

After a dance class, I would buy a bottle of milk at the train station kiosk and drink it all at once. On the train, I felt refreshed although I was very sweaty. I would ride the Oimachi line to the end of Shimotakaido station. Passing through Wakabayashi from Shimotakaido to Sangenjaya station, it was a two-car train. Since it is from one end of the train line to the other, for more than 40 minutes, I did not have to worry about missing my station. I memorized all the things I had learned that day and wrote it all down in my notebook. I concentrated intensely, wanting to "strike while the iron was hot."

ひと針ひと針

　踊りを始めたころ、私の親しい人々は口々に

　「なんか目がパチっと開いてきた。前はなんか半開きで魚みたいな目だったけど」

　とか

　「アンタ、踊りの話始めたら目がキラキラしてくるわ」（関西弁）

　などと言われ、自分でもそれまでドロッとしていた脳みそが、にわかに滝のような勢いで活性化しているのを感じていた。

　誰かに質問されて、じっと考えて答えたのは、学ぶということの喜びを生まれて初めて感じた、から。生まれたての赤ンボのように私は、見るもの聞くものすべてを吸い取った。

　一番最初に、この踊りに引きつけられていったのはいったいどんなふうだったのだろうと思いかえしていた。この踊りのことはまったく知らなかったし、踊り手になろうなどとまったくまったく思っていなかった。

　気がついたのは、自分にとっては本当はそんなに劇的な変化ではな

かったということだ。小さい頃から絵を描くことが好きだったし、いつも描いていた。それで芸術の大学にすすんだ。

　その学校を選んだのは、日本刺繍を習えるのは、そこが日本でただ一つの場所だったからだ。

　日本刺繍を選んだのは、一見古風とも見られるし、日本刺繍が芸術のひとつとはだれも考えないけれども、だけど仏教美術にかかわる主要なもので、実に長い歴史があるからだった。

　東京の国立美術館で「天寿国繍帳」というもっとも古い刺繍の掛物の一部を見た。刺繍で刺された仏さまの絵。美術館の中の暗い狭いすみっこで、なかばかくれていて、気がつかないで通り過ぎてしまってもおかしくない場所だった。

　ものすごい衝撃を受けた。その細かさに、月で踊る兎、壺から立ち昇る煙──その兎や煙はまるで動いているようだった。真ん中には、仏さま。平和なお顔、「完全なる聖性」をそなえて生きている　仏さまが座っていた。

左上：姉の結婚式で　**Left top:** At Asako's sister's wedding, 10/10/1983.
左下：母と　**Left below:** With her mother, 1997 or earlier.
右上：「マヌー」とチャイティとリハーサル　**Right top:** Rehearsing "Divya Kundala Hara Mangalacharan" (choreographed by Guru Gangahdar Pradhan) with Sri Manoranjan Pradhan and Chaitee Sengupta, 2003.
右下：弟子チャイティと　**Right below:** With her student Chaitee.

そこに油絵では感じたことのない、力強い魂を感じた。これはなにか
しら？　「ひと針、ひと針」刺していくのに、気の遠くなるほどの時間
がかかっただろうに。長い時間をかけて創ったその人の、深い献身の念
と祈り…

　たぶん、「ちょっとかじってみるだけでも」いいから、私は「それ」（超
越的なるもの）を経験してみたかったのだろうと思う。そして、大学で
刺繍を習っているときにそこの小さな教室でインド舞踊を見た。
　インド舞踊を始める、それが私の道だった。素材として自分の身体に、
「ひと針ひと針」縫っている、絹の布に刺すかわりに。

Hito hari hito hari (One stitch at a time)

When I started dancing, my close friends observed a change in me:
"Your eyes are brightly open now. They were somewhat half open before, like fish eyes."

And another friend said,

"When you start talking about dance, your eyes sparkle." (in West Japan Kansai dialect).

I also felt my brain had been somewhat slow and dull in the past, but now it was active and vigorous, like a waterfall suddenly flowing.

When somebody asked me questions, I thought thoroughly and in depth. It was the first time that I ever felt the joy of learning, since I was born. Like a newborn baby, I absorbed everything that I watched and heard in class.

Initially, I'd had no desire to be a dancer. I didn't know anything about Indian dance at all. I remember the events that led me to be drawn to this dance form. I loved drawing since I was a small child and I drew all the time. So I decided to go to college to study the fine arts. I chose one school which was the only place in Japan that I could also study Japanese embroidery. This subject was so old fashioned that it wasn't even considered as an art form. But, I chose this subject because it had a long history as one of the art forms related to the Buddhist arts.

In the National Art Museum in Tokyo, I had seen a part of the oldest embroidery, a hanging scroll named "Tenjukoku shuuchou" Mandala. It was a piece of an embroidered Buddha painting. It was housed in a dark, small corner of the museum, almost hidden. One could easily pass by without recognizing it.

I was blown away by it's detail. There was a rabbit dancing on the moon with smoke coming out from a pot which looked so realistic. Buddha was sitting with a peaceful face, looking alive and absolutely sacred.

I was moved by the beauty of the embroidery more than I ever was

Photographed by Bob Giles

with oil paintings for example. I wondered how much work must have gone into this. An enormous amount of time must have been spent on this work: "hito hari hito hari" (one stitch at a time). It was amazing to think of the person who had put in the hours and devotion into this work of art.

I wanted to experience even a small part of this "transcendence." And it was while I was studying the subject of embroidery, that I watched my first Indian dance performance which took place in a small classroom in my college.

I would come to realize that learning Indian dance was my actual calling. It was as if my body was the material to work "hito hari hito hari", one stitch at a time much like stitching on a silk cloth.

オディッシー

　オディッシーダンスは、インド東部、オリッサ地方で踊られていた宗教舞踊だ。ヒンドゥ教の聖地であるこの地には、10世紀前後に建てられたジャガンナート寺院をはじめ、たくさんの寺院がある。オディッシーは、これらの寺院の中で神に捧げる踊りとして生まれた。踊り手は「マハリー」と呼ばれ、その踊り子自身が神と結婚するという形で寺院に暮らし、一日中、神に捧げるためだけに踊っていた。16世紀に、イスラムの支配下に入ると、マハリーは宮廷などにも仕えるようになった。寺院の外に出たオディッシーは、「ゴティプア」という女装した少年の踊り手によって受け継がれ、祝い事の席などで踊られる大衆芸能となるが、イギリス統治時代にはそれも衰退の一途を辿る。独立後1950年代に、何人かのゴティプアにより舞台芸術として復元され、今では古典舞踊の一つとなってインドで親しまれている。

　クラスでクムクムさんは、踊りの動き、理論的なことと共に、折にふれ、インド舞踊の中に流れる宗教、哲学、神話について話してくれた。その話を聞くたびに、私は目の前の世界が宇宙に拡がっていくようでドキドキした気持ちになっていた。彼女は、この踊りを踊る上で一番大切

なのは、いつでも「捧げる」気持ちで踊ることだと繰り返し教えてくれた。稽古場で、彼女が練習用の黄色い木綿のサリーを着て踊り始めると、たちまちガランとした部屋の空気は濃く甘く匂い、その姿は淡い光に包まれて見え、それは私の中に悲しいような、満ち足りたような、あるいは、力がつきあげてくるような様々な感情を一度に巻き起こしながら私をカラッポにした。

　クムクムさんの師、グル　ケルチャラン　モハパトラはオディッシーの第一人者のひとりだ。グルジーはインドの国から「パドマ　ビブーシャン賞」を受賞した、それは日本で言えば人間国宝のようなものだ。とても印象的だったのは、車で移動中、見渡す限り続くオリッサの平らな土地に、ポツポツと浮かぶ小さな鎮守の森のようなものが見えるたびに、大きな河を渡る前、渡り終えるたびに、彼が手を合わせて祈っていたこと。車の中にいる間中、ほとんどその行為を繰り返しているといった感じだった。グルジーのその、月や星、樹や河に対する自然な祈りに触れ、私は私の日常の中にある宇宙を感じたらいいんだなぁと心を揺すられた思いがした。
　夕焼けの空がきれいでうっとりすること雑草がいきおいよく伸びている姿を見る時、毎日生活する中で、この宇宙のすべてのものに感謝することが、オディッシーの底に流れているものだと感じる。

プロデビュー 1984年10月21日、増上寺インド祭り
Her professional debut at Indian Festival at Zojoji temple hall, 10/21/1984.
Photographed by Ryosen Kono

Odissi

Odissi dance originated in the eastern India state of Orissa. There are a lot of temples in this area, including the Jagannath Temple of Puri, built around the 10th century. Odissi dance was originally a temple dance, born from a devotion to the God in these temples. The dancers were known as "Mahari dancers". Mahari dancers lived in the temple as servants of the deity. They did not marry, considering themselves married to the deity of the temple. In the 16th century, under Mughal rule, Maharis were also connected to the court, palace and the king. Odissi dance also became popular entertainment outside the temples, performed by little boys known as "Gotipua dancers". They dressed up in women's clothing and danced at celebrations etc. However, under British rule, the Mahari temple dance faded, as the British and Indian nationals objected to dance in places of worship. The patronage needed for the livelihood of the Mahari dancers was removed. After India's independence, in the 1950s, the dance was restored again as a performing art by some

Photographed by Bob Giles

dance scholars and Gurus. Odissi subsequently became one of the classical dance forms, loved throughout India.

In her class, Kumkum ji talked about dance movement and the theory of Odissi dance. She explained the themes of religion, philosophy and mythology that were an intrinsic part of Indian dance. Every time I heard these stories, I felt my world opening up before me. Kumkum ji emphasized the need to dance Odissi with dedication and feeling. In the class room, when she started dancing in her yellow, practice, cotton saree, there would be a sudden thick sweetness in the air and I felt that Kumkum ji was surrounded by a subtle light or glow. I felt a mixture of emotions; somewhat sad; at the same time, content; and then, I felt a powerful energy from within.

Kumkum ji's own teacher was Guru Kelucharan Mohapatra, one of Odissi's eminent gurus. He received the Padma Vibhushan award, which is the second highest civilian award in India, given for exceptional and distinguished service. I remember his prayers for nature even when we were riding in a car. I watched him as he put his hands together in prayer whenever we saw a grove of trees just looked like trees for any village shrine in Japan, or whenever we passed across a river, for the moon, and the stars. He repeated this action. This touched my heart. I began to think that I just needed to feel the universe in my own daily life. For instance, I wanted to savor the feeling of being enthralled when the sky at sunset was beautiful; or even just appreciate the weeds and plants growing well. I came to realize that this was at the core of Odissi dance.

インド

　私がインドに行っていたのは 1980 年代後半から 90 年代半ばぐらい
まで。82 年に初めてインドをぐるりとカルカッタからカンニャクマリ、
ボンベイと海岸沿いに旅行した。だいたいその後はデリーのクムクムさ
んち。

　この 4 ヶ月間という化学療法、自分の体と向き合っていく際、この本
を書くことで、私の中で化石のように埋もれていた記憶が、光のような
喜びとともに、
　　　「時」というもの
　　　「記憶」というもの
　　　「肉体」というもの
　　　「命」というもの
といっしょによみがえってくる。

　どこに向かう汽車の中だったか。
　私はインドの汽車の開きっぱなしのドアーのところにいた。大きく四
角く切られた空間は、風とともに流れてゆく景色。踏切で止まる車、自

転車、人々が大きな川を渡る、船、白金の草原、小さな村々、てすりに
つかまってその大きく開かれた世界を見る。びゅんびゅんと顔に髪にぶ
つかるあったかい空気。好き。何時間でもずっと立っててあきない。

　ある駅から靴磨きの少年が乗ってくる。何歳？　…7歳くらいかな。
身体は小さいけれど顔がまるで大人のような表情で、遠くからまじまじ
と見てしまった。そして顔色が黄色っぽく、目の下はくまでふくらんで、
髪は黄色くかたくボサボサに固まっている。椅子と椅子、客席と客席の
間に忙しく立ち回り、革靴を履いたおじさんの足元に、小さくしゃがん
で靴を磨き始める。手際よく、ていねいに、完璧な職人技だった。私は
小学生のころ、家の靴磨きをよくやった。父に頼まれて朝、父の黒い革
靴を磨く。ぴかぴかになるのが好きで、よくやった。見ているうちに、
いくらもらうのかな、この仕事で、と思う。彼の姿勢、とにかくとても
きっちりとどこか誇り高いような仕事ぶりなのだ。終わってコインを数
枚、手渡される。手のひらのお金を見て、もうちょっと要求しているよ
うな短いやりとり。おじさんは知らんふりしている。彼はあきらめて列
車と列車の間の方へと歩いていく。私はチャッパルをはいてるから彼に
靴磨きを頼めないけれど、その彼に敬意を表していくらかさしあげたい
とあとを追う。近づいたところで、トイレからおじさんが出てきた。手
をポケットに入れた拍子にお札がパラリ。靴磨きの子は脱兎のような素

76

Photographed by Ryosen Kono

早さでそれをひろった。そして私がそれを見ちゃったのをみとめ、上目づかいの固い表情で私をじっと見返した。私はとっさに

「やったね、ラッキーじゃん」

と心の中で叫んで、にかーっと笑った。

彼の笑いかえす顔、白い歯がこぼれて、本当に嬉しそうにする。子どもの笑い顔だった。そしてさっと汽車から飛び降りて行った。ずっと前のことだけど今も時々、彼の顔を思い出す。仕事をしている真剣な顔、でも疲れた大人のひとの表情で、そして残していった子どもの笑い顔。

India

I went to India from the late 1980s to the mid 1990s. In 1982, I first traveled around India from Kolkata to Kanyakumari; Bombay and along the coast. After that I went to Kumkum ji's in Delhi.

I have been going through chemotherapy for the last 4 months. When I face my body, and continue the writing of this book, the memories that were buried like fossils in me, come alive with joy and light:

With "time",

"Memory",

"Body",

"Life",

The memories come back.

Where was the train going?

I was at the door of the train in India. The view was visible through a large square door which was kept opened. The landscape flowed by with the wind. There were cars, bicycles and people waiting at a railway crossing. The train crossed a big river with boats. There were platinum grasslands, small villages, small cows. I held onto the handles of the train and watch the vast open world. The warm air hit my face and hair. I liked everything about this feeling. I could never get bored, standing like this for hours.

A boy who cleaned people's shoes to earn money, got on the train. How old could he possibly be? ... Only about seven years old perhaps? As I was staring at him from a distance, I noticed that his body was small but his face looked grown-up. It looked yellowish. His under eye area was swollen. His hair was yellow and hardened. He busily walked around between the chairs, the box and the box seating. He started polishing shoes with a crouching crawl at the foot of the gentlemen who wore leather shoes. He was demonstrating that he was polishing efficiently and carefully with perfect craftsmanship. When I was an elementary school child, I did a lot of shoe polishing at home. My father asked me to brush his black leather shoes in the morning. I liked the shoes to become shiny. I did it well. I wondered how much this little boy was going to get from this work. His posture showed how proudly he worked. When he finished, several coins were handed over to him. Looking at the money in his palm, there was a brief interaction with the customer, requesting a bit more. The gentleman ignored the request. The boy gave up and walked towards the area between the cars of the train. I could not ask him to polish for me because I was wearing chappals (sandals). But I thought that I would follow him and hand him some money to show him my respect for his work. As I approached him, a gentleman came out of the bathroom. A bill fell from his pocket when he pulled his hand out. The boy quickly got it from the floor. The boy noticed that I had seen what had happened and he was gazing at me with a firm look in his eyes. Without thinking,

"You did it. Lucky you!"

I cried in my heart and gave him a big smile. His face smiling back at me, with white teeth, made me really happy. It was the smiling face of a child. Then, he quickly jumped out off the train. It happened a long time ago, but I still remember his face. A serious working face, but with a look of a tired adult. The memory of his laughing face as a child stays with me.

Photographed by Ryosen Kono

ケルチャラン モハパトラ グルジーの東京ワークショップ

　86年にクムクムさんがグルジーを日本に招待し、集中ワークショップを受けた時のことを思い出した。もう20年も前のことになっちゃったので、おそらく殺気立ってたであろうそのときのことも、今では胸がぎゅっとなるような思い出に変わっている。そしてそれは、まさしく私の踊り人生のなかでも飛躍的な瞬間のひとつだった。クムクムさんは、

　「あなたたちは、とってもラッキーです。」

　と、繰り返し言ってたけれど、日本で習い始めてまだ3年程の私には、その意味がわかろうはずもなく、床に座ってチャイをすすっている小柄な老人（60代前半）を遠巻きにながめていました。そのあと、インドに行って初めてその言葉の意味を理解したけれど。

　グルジーからその時習ったのは、シャンカラバラナム パラヴィ。クムクムさんが、その演目は難しすぎます、と言うのもおかまいなしに、グルジーはすっと立ち上がり、出だしの動きを見せた。…それは、その瞬間は、私の眼にやきついて、そして、一生私の目から離れることはないと思う。

「小柄なおじいさん」の肢体は、官能的な香りを放ちつつ、「美」、そのものに変容してしまった。真実を内包する美。直接ハートに飛び込んでくる真実。言葉にすると、どうもピンとこないけど。

　それは、83年に初めてサンジュクタさんの踊りを見たときから始まっていたオディッシーの旅の道しるべ、「奥の細道」をゆく道をしめす瞬間だったと思う。そして、ここまで書いて、その機会を与えてくれたクムクムさんと、深く輝くような秘密を見せてくれたグルジーに、有難い気持がこみ上げてきた。

　グルジーのクラスの合間の休み時間、窓際で、ほてった体を、湿ったサリーのひんやりで涼めつつ、夜の空を眺めると、低く三日月が出て、そのすぐ下にヴィーナスが大きく輝いている。うぁっ、きれい。幸せだなぁと眺めてると、となりにグルジーがいて、グルジーは、その首から下がるルードラクシャ（菩提樹の実に紐を通した数珠）を両手の間にはさみ、その月と、星に、祈っている。その横顔は、「これがこの踊りの真髄」と静かに私に言っていた。トルソーの動き、正確なターラ（拍子）、すべての技術の奥にさらさらと流れ続けているもの。

　シャンカラバラナムに話が戻るが、毎日のクラスで習ったことを、次

の日までにきちんと覚えて踊れるようにしていくために、クラスが終わったとたん、ノートに習ったことをメモするけれど、今まで見たこともない複雑な動きの上、とても長い一連の振り付けを一度に覚えなくてはならない。空白な部分が出てくる。ああでもない、こうでもないと記憶を辿る。家に戻る電車の中、歩いてる途中——。そして家に帰ると小さな台所でノートを片手に練習。気がつくと夜の３時、４時になっている。でも納得がいくまで、覚えるまでは、寝られないもんね。私の人生であんなにも私の頭脳がアップルコンピュータのように起動したことはなかった。クラスの間は、グルジーのすべての動きを目から飲み込んで、あとで組み立てていく。必死だったけど、私はその間ずっと、空からお花の花びらが私の頭に降ってきてるようなしあわせを感じていました。祝福、というのかね。

　しかし、シャンカラバラナムを終え、グルジーが、シバ神のシュロカ（お祈り）を私たちのために特別（クムクムさん、とてもラッキーです、と、また）に一曲振り付けしてくれるころには、もうすっかり燃え尽きていて、どうやっても、振り付けが覚えられなかった。
　クムクムさんの話、グルジーの話、もっともっと聞いてもらいたい。
　そして、「伝統芸術」についても。ずっと私の中にあったその問いは、今この砂漠の山での実験的、試行錯誤と、私というフィルターをとおし

て、ちらちら見え隠れ。

　こうして思い出すこと、書くことが、今そのための大切なプロセスに
なっています。
　聖なる踊りのドキュメンタリーの映画を作るプロジェクトが始まっ
て、ここ数日、撮影をしています。まずは10分ほどのものを作って、
いろいろなプロダクションに送るのだそうです。時間かかりそうだけど、
エクサイティング。

　（アリゾナの仏教リトリートセンターに滞在中に書かれた／編者註）

上：クムクム ジーのクラス
Top: A snap from Kumkum ji's class.
右：ケルチャラン グルジーと。
Rigth: With Kelucharan Guruji.

Kelucharan Mohapatra Guruji's Tokyo Workshop

In 1986, Kumkum ji invited Guru Kelucharan Mohapatra, to Japan. I clearly remember this intensive workshop. Twenty years have passed by since that time, so it is entirely possible that, things that may have been frantic at the time in the workshop, have now turned into fond memories that make my heart ache sweetly. But it was exactly in this workshop, that I experienced a huge leap in my dance. Kumkum ji told us,

"You all are very lucky."

She repeatedly said it. Yet, I had only learned Odissi dance for 3 years in Japan, so I at first, I could not fully understand what she meant. I watched from a distance, this rather small, old man, sitting on the floor, drinking chai. I came to truly understand the meaning of Kumkum ji's word, only after I went to India myself.

From Guruji's workshop, I learned Shankarabharanam Pallavi. Kumkum ji said this item would be too difficult for the group but without paying any attention to that, Guruji stood up and showed one movement from the beginning of the item. That moment was imprinted onto my eyes and never left for the rest of my life.

The limbs of the little, old man were transformed into movements of beauty; beauty that encompasses the truth. This truth jumps directly into one's heart. I cannot express the feeling in words.

It was this moment in my life that I found the path for my Odissi journey, "Oku no Hosomichi." The journey had already begun when I had seen Sanjukta's performance for the first time in 1983. And, as I wrote until this point, I was so grateful to Kumkum ji for giving me this opportunity in dance. Now I was grateful to Guruji for showing me the truth of the deeply shining secret, which filled within me.

During the break time between Guruji's classes, I remember once, standing by the window, cooling down my warm body with my damped saree and looking at the night sky. The low crescent moon appeared and Venus shined greatly beneath it. Wow, it was beautiful! I was feeling so much happiness. Guruji was next to me. He was praying to the moon and the stars, with his rudraksha necklace of beads between his hands (rudraksha is a rosary stringed through fruits of linden trees). The profile of his face quietly told me, "This is the essence of this dance."

It is continuously flowing deeply within us, underneath all the technique of torso movement; accurate taala (beat) and so on.

As soon as the class finished, I made notes on what I learned in Shankarabharanam Pallavi, so that by the next day I would be able to dance properly in the workshop. I had to memorize a very long sequence of the choreography at once. I had not seen some of these complicated movements before. Sometimes I would draw a blank: is the step like this or is it more like that? I would engage my memory as I was walking, and riding the train back home. And when I got home, I practiced with my notes in my hand in my small kitchen. It would pass 3 a.m. and sometimes even 4 a.m. But until I felt

アリゾナ州の仏教リトリートセンターで。2005年
At the Buddhist retreat center in Arizona, 2005.

convinced I knew it, I could not go to sleep. In my life, so much of my brain never really worked efficiently like an Apple computer. Yet during class, I would take in and absorb every movement of Guruji with my eyes and would assemble it all later in my mind. Although I felt desperate to learn, I also felt a happiness that felt a little like flower petals falling continuously from the sky. I felt blessed.

When we finished Shankarabharanam, I was already completely burned out. Guruji choreographed Lord Shiva's Sloka (a prayer) for us especially. Kumkum ji again said, "you all are very lucky". Somehow, I cannot remember the choreography at all now, no matter how hard I try and remember.

I would like to keep recounting my stories of Kumkum ji and Guruji more and more. I would also like to recount my stories about "these traditional arts." Now at this trying time in my life, I feel glimpses of them.

Recalling and writing this way is now an important process for that purpose.

There is also a project to make a movie of the sacred dance, a documentary film. They are shooting films on my dance these days. First of all, they are going to make about a 10 minute piece to send to various producers. It seems that it will take time but I am excited.

(Written while staying at the Buddhist Retreat Center in Arizona / editor's note).

ブバネシュワールへのバスの旅

　バスは道路から浮かんでるかというスピードで、藪の続く白茶けた荒野や、睡蓮の浮かぶ湿地帯を貫いて一本道を飛ばす。バスが急ブレーキをかけて止まり、土ぼこりの中に降り立つと目の前には小さなチャイ屋さん、バスの騒音とスピードから放り出されると、そこはしんとして音のない昼の明るい日射しのなかである。小さな羽虫の群が黄金色に光っている。地面におかれた木のテーブルの上に、屋根のヤシの葉の間から洩れた光が模様をつくってゆれている。そこに坐って甘ーいチャイを飲んでひと休みする。

The Bus Trip to Bhubaneswar.

The bus was going at high speed almost floating off the surface of the road. It went on a long, single street through the wilderness with the faded color bushes and also through the wetlands where the water lilies float. When the bus stopped suddenly, I got off in the dust. There, I found a small chai shop in front of me. Away from the noise and speed of the bus, I found myself in the bright sunlight in the daytime with no sound. A group of small insects were shining in golden light. Light filtered between the leaves of the palm trees and reflected off the roof created patterns on the wooden table on the ground. People sat at the table for a break and drank sweet chai.

Photographed by Bob Giles

ケルチャラン グルジー

　グルジーは待っていた——というよりは、「待ってるポーズ」で坐っていた。その美しい村の大きな樹の下で。グルジーは自分の生まれた村、ラーガラージプールに、大きなお寺を建立していた。もうだいぶできてきたころ、私はその村ラーガラージプールを訪ねた。

　ラーガラージプールはブバネシュワールからプリーに向かうハイウェイ（の中の一本道）の途中にあり、ハイウェイから高いヤシの樹々に囲まれた細い土手道を歩いて行くと、突然目の前にからんと村が開ける。広場のような村の真ん中には大きなバミヤン樹がそびえ立っているのが見える。その両脇には高床式の縁側のある家が並んでいる。広い河のほとりに、ヤシの樹の葉が空高くゆれている、ひっそりとしてひだまりの民がそこここにいるような小さな村だった。

　グルジーの家は石像を彫る職人だったと聞いたけど、この村はパタチットラというオリッサ独特の絵師のいる村だった。村の真ん中に大きな大きな樹がそびえている。この村の鎮守さま、まるで村全体をおおう

ように。

　大きな樹の近くの軒下で、グルジーはミニアチュールの絵のクリシュナのように坐っていた。片膝を立て、薄いドーティーがふわりとその立てた膝を覆い、片腕でその上体をささえて、もう一方の腕は立てた膝に長く、ゆるやかにのっている。

　いつだったか、グルジーが話してくれた、あの神さまかと思った。
　それは、グルジーが小さかった頃（3、4才といったか？）すごい病気にかかり、高熱の中、生死をさまよっていたことがある。グルジーのお母さんはこの樹の神さまの元に一晩中座って（マー　ブアシュニ女神）に願をかけて、この子を助けてくださいと祈った。今があるのもこの神さまが命を救ってくれたおかげだと。この女神さまに感謝の念とともに、お寺を建立した。
　まだ、足場は渡っているけれども、この部分は自分で作った、あとはここにそれを入れてと話しながらいろいろと説明をしてくれる。お寺は完成してグルジーの命を救った女神さまにりっぱな家を建てたあと、グルジーは2004年に他界した。まさに天寿を全うするというのはこういうことなのね。

Photographed by Ryosen Kono

　きっちりと人生を生きた人だとつくづく思う。グルジーのような人に生で接する機会があったことだけでも、私は私の人生に感謝するに値すると感じている。

Kelucharan Guruji

Guruji was waiting — in other words, he was literally sitting in "waiting pose," under the big tree of that beautiful village. In those days, Guruji was building a big temple in his own village, Raghurajpur. When the construction was almost completed, I visited the village of Raghurajpur.

Raghurajpur is located in the middle of the highway heading from Bhubaneshwar to Puri. When I was walking the narrow bank of the road surrounded by high palm trees from the highway, suddenly the village appeared in an open space. In the middle of the village, there was a plaza, where I saw a large banyan tree standing tall. On both sides of the tree, there were houses with raised floor margins with wooden strips or "engawa." On the banks of a large river, I saw the leaves of the palm trees swaying high in the sky. The village was in a quiet, sunny spot. There were villagers hanging out here and there.

I heard that in Guruji's household there was a craftworker who

Photographed by Bob Giles

sculpted stone statues. This village was known for Orissa's distinctive painting called Patachitra. The big, big tree rose in the middle of the village as if it were the guardian of the village, covering the whole village.

Under the leaves near the big tree, Guruji was sitting like a miniature painting of Lord Krishna. One knee was bent and one was in the sitting position. He wore a thin dhoti. He was leaning his upper body on one arm, and the other loosely stretched arm was resting gently on the bent knee.

I thought this was a temple for the God that Guruji talked about.

When Guruji was small (about 3 or 4 years old perhaps), he became extremely ill. He had a very high fever. Guruji's mother sat at the Goddess (Ma Bhuasunii) of this tree all night and prayed. Please help this boy she prayed. To thank this Goddess who saved his life, he built this temple. Although the scaffolds were still there, crossing, he explained the structure, talking about putting in this part and then putting in another part there. The temple was eventually completed. Guruji passed away in 2004 after building a fine home for the Goddess who saved his life. That's exactly how one should live his natural life.

I truly believe that Guruji was a person who lived his life properly. Since I had the opportunity to meet someone like Guruji, I give gratitude for my life.

Photographed by Bob Giles

ブバネシュワール ミシュラ ジー

　背のヌーっと高く、四角いガッチリした体に大きくてこれまた四角い顔、ごつそうな、それが私の第一印象だった。しかし人柄は温厚で控えめでいらした。

　クムクム モハンティーさんちのパーティで。ケルチャラン グルジーが来るまでミシュラ ジーは食事に手を付けない。みなそれぞれ食事が出て各々食べ始めてた。私は食べ物を口に運ぶのを止めて、へーっといたく感心した。私がベジタリアンだというと、
　「一週間に一回チキンを食べるのは悪くないよ」
　と言われた。私は守らなかったけど。

　何よりも一番印象に残っているのは、ブバネシュワールに着いてまだ日の浅いころ、ミシュラ ジーを訪ねることにした。まだ右も左もわからず、グルジーやみんながどこにいるのかもわからずに日を暮らしていた。一刻も早く踊りを始めたい一心でいた。もらった住所を頼りにリキシャのおじさんに連れていってもらう。どのくらい遠いのか、地理感覚

ゼロ。とにかく連れてってもらうしかない。

　辺りは夕暮れからだんだん薄闇、家々の灯りが灯ってくる。土手（？）のような道を行き、団地のような建物が並んでいるのがみえる。えーっここかなあ。間違ってんじゃないの？　まさかミシュラ ジーが団地に住んでいようとは思ってなかった。

　すると、トロトロとかすかに聴こえるあのヴァイオリンの音。暗い。すっかり夜となった中であの美しい音色をたどっていく。なんて、なんて、ロマンチックだった。次第に近づくその音色。団地の中に入り、階段をのぼり、小さなアパートにミシュラ ジーは座ってヴァイオリンを奏でていた。まさに、クリシュナのフルートに誘われて森をさまようゴーピー（牛飼い娘）の気持ちがちょっぴりわかったような瞬間だった。

　ブバネシュワール ミシュラ ジーは、インドでも最も功績の高いバイオリニストであり、作曲家で、ケルチャラン グルジーがオディッシーの父ならば、ミシュラ ジーはオディッシーの母であるとも言える。

Photographed by Ryosen Kono

Bhubaneswar Mishra ji

He was a tall man, with a bit of a square shaped body. He was a calm and modest person.

At a party at Kumkum Mohanty's house, Mishra ji did not touch the meal in front of him, until Kelucharan Guruji arrived. The meal was served and the rest of us had started eating. But I stopped putting the food in my mouth, because I was so impressed by Mishra ji's gesture in waiting for Guruji. When I told him that I was a vegetarian, he said,

"It is not bad to eat chicken once a week."

I have not followed this advice though.

Something that clearly stayed in my memory was this. Shortly after I arrived in Bhubaneswar, I decided to visit Mishra ji. I still did not know where to go, either to the right or the left, living my days without knowing where Guruji and everyone were. I wanted to start dancing as soon as possible. I had to rely on the given address written on a piece of paper, to have the rickshaw driver take me to Mishra ji's house. How far was it? I had no geographical sense. I had no other choice but to trust him to get me there.

It was getting gradually dark in the evening. The lights of the houses came on. The driver took me along a road by the side of an embankment. I could see that there were apartment complexes lined up. Is it okay here? Is it the right place? Somehow, I did not expect Mishra ji to live in an apartment complex.

Then, the sound of that violin reached me faintly in the dark. I followed that beautiful sound since it was now night. Oh, the sound was awe inspiring and romantic. The sound became closer and closer gradually. I entered one of the buildings, climbed the stairs, and found Mishra ji sitting in a small apartment, playing the violin. It was that moment that I understood a little, the feelings of the gopis (milkmaids), wandering in the forest when Krishna's flute sounded. Bhubaneswar Mishra ji was one of the most prolific violinists and composers in India. If Kelucharan Guruji can be called the father of Odissi, Bhubaneswar Mishra ji would be the mother of Odissi.

Photographed by Bob Giles

河むこうの トリナート マハラナ ジー

「クムクムさん、私、パッカワージ習いたいんですけど」
　ずっと、胸の内にあってなかなか行動に出来なかったことをついに口にした。グルジーが日本に来て、パッカワージ（太鼓）を叩きまくる（？）姿に血が躍り、ぜったい習うゾと自分に誓ってから何年かたっていた。
「パッカワージを習得するには踊りと同じくらい身を入れてやらないとダメダ。一日中タイコの前に坐って練習し続けるくらいでないとゼッタイうまくなんねえ…そんなら踊りの練習はいつすることになるのか…」

　始める前からそんなことで躊躇していた。でもパッカワージを習い出して、それまで聴いていたオディッシーの音楽が、そしてパッカワージ

のリズムと踊りの動きの関係が全く違って見えてきて、びっくりするほど新鮮な発見だった。興奮しながらそれまで習った一曲一曲の踊りを新しい気持ちで踊っていたことを憶えている。

　クムクムさんはすぐに、彼女の知っている何人かのパッカワージ奏者に連絡をとってくれ、私はトリナート　マハラナ　ジーという方から太鼓を習うことになった。マハラナ　ジーはオリッサ出身で、お兄さんはボンベイにいて、二人ともオディッシーの踊りの先生である。

Photographed by Bob Giles

Trinath Maharana ji across the river

"Kumkum ji, I would like to learn the pakhawaj."

I finally told her what I had in my heart. When Guruji came to Japan, I saw that he played his pakhawaj drum on and on, with full strength. It made my heart leap with joy, and I made a pact to myself that I would also learn the pakhawaj. A few years already had passed since then. In order to learn pakhawaj, I had to put in all my effort just as in dance, otherwise it wouldn't work. I thought to myself that, I wouldn't be able play pakhawaj well, unless I sat in front of the drum all day long to practice. But then, when would I be able to practice dance?

I was hesitant with such an endeavor even before I started. And yet, I started learning the pakhawaj. The music of Odissi I had been listening to thus far felt very different. The relationship between the rhythm of the pakhawaj and the dancer's movements felt also very different. It was a surprisingly fresh discovery for me. I was excited to be dancing with a new feeling about the songs that I had learned.

Kumkum ji had contacted some of the pakhawaij players she knew. I decided to learn the drumming from Trinath Maharana ji. Trinath Maharana ji is from Orissa and his older brother was in Bombay. Both of them were Odissi dance teachers.

康 米那さん
かん　み　な

　在日韓国人として大阪に生まれる。たしか私より 12 才上のねずみ年。そうすると今は 58 才。英国人のパートナー、デッド ホルスト氏。温和なまなざしのビートニク ジェネレーション。バイクに乗っていた。前の奥さんと子ども（娘さん？）が英国にいる。当時の生徒の間の噂では貴族の出とか…。米那さんが踊る時に、左手の薬指に光る指輪、照明に照らされてとても美しくキラッ、キラッと光っていて、私は光り物に興味が全くなかったのにもかかわらず、いいなあキレイだなあっと見ていた。踊りのときにこういうふうに光るものが手や手首にあるといいもんだなぁなんて考えていたんだ。

　なんでそんなこと覚えてんのかね。おもしろい。だってそれはおそらくたった一日のあるパフォーマンスのことで、それ以外のぎっしりとつまった思い出に比べたら、「その他」の部類のことなのに。とにかくそんなふうに「記憶」というものはおもしろい。私の場合、ゴチャゴチャの机の引き出しみたいにはいっている。開けてみて最初に目についた小っちゃな丸くなったケシゴム、端っこのほうにへばりついた三角定規、

あれ何探してんだっけ？　こうして米那さんのことを書くのは私の記憶の引き出しを整理して、米那さんが私の人生を大きく変えた存在であることを改めて認識し、感謝するための作業。

　イリアナ チトラスチさんの書いたグルジーの本は、彼女のグルジーに対しての愛と感謝が一番美しくパワフルな形としての表れだと私は感じる。どこか使命のような強い意志をもっている。(*The Making of a Guru Kelucharan Mohapatra His Life and Times*) by Ileana Citrasti [Masnohar])

　私の場合、たった今、米那さんに関して思いつくことをすべて書いてみる。まずはそれをやってみる。

　79年か、80年。

　通っていた学校でみたインド舞踊。リーラ サムソンとマーダヴィ ムドゥガル。その頃の、インドの若手（30代前半）舞踊家二人が小さなクラスルームに来た。ガランとした殺風景な部屋に、たくさんのジュエリーで身体全体をおおい、足には鈴をつけて、どんな踊りをどのくらいやったかちーっとも覚えていない。ワークショップの最後に集まった生徒20〜30人と記念写真を撮る時も、私は「記念写真なんて…」と坐ったままで眺めていた。今、振り返ると、そんな写真に写っている自分を見てみたかったような。

Photographed by Ryosen Kono

　タマちゃんか誰かといっしょに観たのか、それとも一人で観てタマちゃんに話したのか、誰かといっしょに観たのかどうかも憶えていない。アートゼミの告知板。それをみてふらりと一人で行ったのだったか。それとも「こんなのがあるよ」と友だちを誘ったのだったか、誘ったけれ

ども誰も来れなくて一人で行ったのか。そしてそのあと、おそらく興奮
して話したのだろう、彼女が雑誌『ぴあ』の催しの欄に載っているイン
ド舞踊のフリーレクチャーデモのことを教えてくれた。けっこうすぐ、
今週の日曜日だ とか。彼女は行けないけれど
　「アサコちゃん行ってみたら？　ただだよ」

　19才だった。よく覚えていない。その学校のゼミの時観たインド舞踊。
そんなに大感動、人生を変えるような体験ではなかったと思うのだが、
私は周りの人々に見た踊りのことを熱っぽく語っていたのだろう。武蔵
境のアパートで。絹ちゃんと住んでた白梅荘。電話でボーイフレンド（っ
ぽい人）に話していたり、吉田雅浩君に手紙でそのことを書いていた、
かもしれない。

　最初の最初の最初のページ。私がその後めくり続ける本の。

　タマちゃん、高木一美さん、埼玉の旅館の娘さん、たまたま名簿で前
の人だったから前に坐っていた人。まじめでおとなしいしっかりとした
お嬢さん。今ごろ、どんな暮らしをしているのか。卒業制作に美しい辻ヶ
花のタンスを作っていた。たまたま前に坐ったタマちゃん（そういうわ
けでタマちゃんと呼んだわけではないけれど）のおかげで、私は康 米

那タゴールダンスを踊る会のフリーレクチャーデモに行き、そのまま踊りを習い始めた。タゴールダンスは、インド　ベンガル地方出身の詩人、ラビンドラナート　タゴールが独自の舞踊を自作の詩に振り付けたもので、インドの最初のモダンダンスとも言われている。劇や人間の感情を自然な感じで表現して、歌と踊りで物語るもの。

　茗荷谷は丸の内線で通っていた学校のある東中野から一本。でも池袋の方はあんまり行ったことがなかった。やはり一人で行った。地図で調べたのか、電話で問い合わせたのか、茗荷谷の駅を降りてくるりと駅を背にして細い坂道を下っていく。国士舘の学生が歩いていたりして古い家並み。

　米那さんの踊りは数週間前に偶然見た踊りとは全く違い、お化粧も派手な衣装も身につけず、上下黒の練習服を着て、長い三つ編みを背中にたらして弥勒菩薩のような細くしなやかな肢体。細面で仏像のような顔。ときどき目を上に上げると、その瞳は弧空の中に何かを見出そうとするようなどこか深い悲しみや憂をたたえていた。

　米那さんの踊りには、命を賭ける戦士のようなものがあった。米那さんは踊りに「命をかけていた」。どこか戦っているような、とりつかれ

たような激しさがあった。私は踊りというよりもそんな彼女に惹かれた。あの瞳が探し求めているのは一体何なのか？　19才になった私に訪れた菩薩様、康 米那さん。

　毎年、冬になると米那さんはインドに踊りを習いに行った。3、4ヶ月、インドで先生から朝から晩まで習い、帰ってくるとなんかひとまわり痩せているようだった。酷使したというのがわかるのである。でも輝いていまも熱を持っているような目で全身から漲るエネルギーを発しつつ、稽古にもますます厳しさが増すようだった。

　踊りを習いに来ていた人々
　　　愛ちゃん 芸大の油絵出てた
　　　紀子さん　もうインドに何回も何回も行っちゃって、ヒンディー語もできて、特別何をやってるかわからないけれど、インドと恋人関係の人。私よりきっと十五才かそれ以上は離れてるかも。誰も歳は知らない。かなり年上の感じがした。
　　　環さん ヒンディ映画を日本に紹介して一躍有名になった。ベンガル語を話す。
　　　久代さん 子どものような人
　　　モスさん ずっと上で近寄り難い感じだったけど、だんだん踊

りを通して仲良くなる。そしてたくさんの人々

ベンガルのバウル（神秘的な歌唱の伝統）研究してた人 タゴール、サタジット レイ（インドの映像作家）などに強い影響をうけてインドに行きびたり

ケララの長編小説を日本に紹介する人

コッラニ月刊誌を発行し続けた人

ゴンド族の女の人と結婚した人

シタール、タブラ、サロッド、カルナータカ ヴォーカルの人たち

ミティラー美術館

インド芸能に精通しているお坊さん

細密画画家

Mina Kang

She was a Korean, born in Osaka, Japan. I think she was born in the year of the rat because I know that she was 12 years older than me. She would probably be 58 years old now. She had a British partner, Ted Holst. He was from the Beatnik generation. He looked at things in a very calm and gentle manner. He rode a motorcycle. His former wife and child (a daughter I think) were back in England. The rumor among the students at that time was that he must have come from one of the noble families in England. On one occasion, as Mina san was dancing on stage, a ring on her ring finger of her left hand, shone beautifully, illuminated by stage lighting. Although I was not that interested in jewelry, I found it to be so beautiful. I thought that it would be nice to have something like that on a hand or wrist while dancing.

Why is it that I remember that particular moment? It is interesting because, it was just one performance on one random day. Anyway, my memories are interesting in that way. They look like the drawer of a desk. While opening the drawer, sometimes, a small rounded eraser would come in to my view first, and then a triangular ruler that stuck to the edge. My memories worked in a similar fashion. Hmm, what was I looking for in my "memories drawer?" Writing about Mina san in this way helps me organize my memory drawer. It helps me to recognize once again how Mina san changed my life greatly, and reminds me that I would like to thank her.

I think Guruji's book written by Ileana Citaristi was a manifestation of Ileana's compassion and appreciation for Guruji, in the most beautiful and powerful form. She had a strong will and a mission. (The book is called, *The Making of a Guru-Kelucharan Mohapatra, His Life and Times.* by Ileana Citaristi. Manohar publishers.) Presently, I would like to remember and write everything that comes up in my memory about Mina san.

The year was 1979 or 1980.

I had just seen an Indian dance performance at the school where I was studying. Leela Samson and Madhavi Mudgal were the dancers. They were two emerging, Indian young dancers (in their early 30s) at that time. They came to our small, bare classroom. Their bodies were adorned with a lot of jewelry and they wore bells on their feet. I do not remember what kind of dance they did or for how long they danced. When someone took a group photo with 20 or 30 students, at the end of the workshop, I sat out at the side. As I watched them, I was thinking to myself, "I'm not so interested in pictures." Looking back now, I wish that I could see myself in such a picture.

I learned of another upcoming Indian dance performance from my friend, Tama chan. I think she told me about this free lecture demonstration of Indian dance, that she'd seen in the column of "Pia" magazine (the entertainment information magazine). Although she could not go with me, she said, "Why don't you go, Asako chan? It is a free event."

I was 19 years old at the time. I didn't think that the performance by the two Indian dancers in my school, had had that much of an impact on me. However, I think that I must have talked passionately about dance to people close to me. I must have talked to my "boyfriend" on the phone about dance and I may have written to Masahiro Yoshida about dance. I was in an apartment named "White plum house" in Musashisakai where I lived with Kinu chan, my sister.

Tama chan, whose full name was Kazumi Takagi san was the daughter of a ryokan in Saitama. She happened to sit in front of me in school. She was serious, quiet and whole hearted. I remember that she made a beautiful Tsujigahana drawer for her graduation project. It was all thanks to Tama chan that I attended the free lecture demonstration of the Tagore dance performed by Mina san. And shortly after that, I started learning dance from her too. The
Bengali poet of India, Rabindranath Tagore had invented a new style of dance choreography. It was seen as the first modern style of dance in India. His approach was to encourage natural expression to convey drama and human emotions. The main characteristic of Tagore's works was that the stories were told entirely through song and dance.

Myogadani on the Marunouchi subway line, it was a direct line from

Higashi Nakano where our school was. However, I hadn't gone to the stations toward Ikebukuro that often. When I got to Myogadani station, I went down the narrow slope leaving the station behind. I noticed some students of Kokushikan University walking around the town.

Mina san's dance was totally different from the dance I had seen a few weeks ago. Mina san did not wear make-up or an elaborate costume. She wore plain, black top and bottoms and had a braid hanging down her back. She was thin with supple limbs like the Miroku Bodhisattva Maitreya. (Bodhisattva is an ordinary person who takes up a course in his/her life that moves them in the direction of Buddha.) Mina san's face was like that of a slender Buddha statue. Sometimes she would raise her eyes, into the sky, with deep sadness and sorrow.

Mina san's dance had a quality akin to a warrior battling for her life. Mina san "gave her life to dance". There seemed to be an unrelenting intensity to her performance. I was attracted to the character of the woman more than her dance itself. I wondered what she was seeking

Photographed by Bob Giles

with her eyes. Mina Kang, was the Bodhisattva who I met at the age of 19 years.

Every year in winter, Mina san went to India to learn dance for 3 or 4 months. She would learn from her teacher all day from morning till night. She seemed to be thinner when she came home. Apparently her body had been through rigorous training. Yet her shining fiery eyes showed only a bright energy. When she returned, her lessons became very serious and powerful more than usual.

The following are people who came to learn dance from her.

Ai chan: graduated from Tokyo National University of Fine Arts and Music majoring in oil painting.

Noriko san: she had already been to India many times. She was able to speak Hindi. I wasn't sure what she was doing especially. She was in love with India. She was about 15 years older than me.

Tamaki san: introduced Hindi movies to Japan and became famous. Tamaki san spoke Bengali.

Hisayo san: seemed very young.

Mosu san: she was much older than me and I couldn't easily talk to her but gradually we got along through dancing.

And there were other students besides these including:

one who was studying Baul (the mysterious singing tradition in Bengal). He was influenced strongly from Tagore and Satyajit Ray (Indian film artist) and went to India all the time.

another person who introduced Kerala's novels to Japan;

one who published "Korha ni" monthly magazine;

one person who was married to a Gond tribe woman;

there were people who were learning sitar, tabla, sarod, Carnatic vocal music;

Mithilar museum

one was a Buddhist monk who was very knowledgeable about the Indian arts;

and a miniature painter.

サンジュクタさんの最期

　アメリカに来てから、だった。97年、サンジュクタさんが逝ってしまっ
たという知らせが届いた。だけど私はどうして、どんなふうにとあれこ
れ調べたり聞いたりしなかった。でも、52才という年齢と、思うよう
に踊れなくて、パフォーマンスのあと、舞台を降りて楽屋で泣いていた
ということを、クムクムさんから聞いていた。ひざの手術をした？　乳
がんだった？　はっきりした情報のないままだった。

　そしてブバネシュワールの家を訪ねた時のことを思い出す——。
　その時、グルジーが
　「サンジューっ！　サンジューっ！」
　と名前を呼びながら家に入っていく、私はグルジーの後について入っ
ていった。
　サンジュクタさんは、グレーの薄い透き通ったサリーを両肩からかけ
て、腕を組み、堂々として表情もくずさず歩いて部屋に入ってきた。ひ
とことも口をきかなかった…。そんな様子が近寄りがたかった。ちょっ
とこわかった、堂々としすぎてて。

サンジュクタさんは舞台の前はコスチュームをすべてつけて30分前には静かに瞑想するということだった。

　病気のことは、誰にも言わなかった。誰も知らなかったとクムクムさんが言っていた。

　もし、みんなが知っていて、みんなの励ましをたくさん受けていた――と思ってしまう。

　オディッシーを世界に知らしめたグルジーの愛弟子。

　私の人生を変えた人。1983年の草月ホールの彼女の踊りを観た日から、私は踊りに魂を捧げてしまった。

　サンジュクタさんは踊りに命をかけて足早に通り抜けていってしまった。52才でガンで逝ってしまった。逝く直前まで誰にもそのことを知らせず、クムクムさんもびっくりしたらしい。
　乳がんが骨に移ったという話を聞いた。サンジュクタさんにとって、もちろんすごい葛藤があっただろうけど、踊れない身体にいる必要は全

Photographed by Ryosen Kono

くなく、あっさりと肉体から離れていったように感じてしまう。

　彼女の踊りによって魂を開かされた人が世界中にどれほどいるだろう
か。その一人である私は1983年草月ホールでの彼女の踊りの中にはっ
きりと「神」というものを見てしまった。そして私の人生はそれまでと
全く変わってしまったのである。なんだかわからない。肉体にあって肉
体にない。しっかりと彼女であって彼女を超えてしまっている。全身か
ら黄金の光が輝きあふれている。完璧にリズムと身体がひとつになって
もう止まらないという感じ。完璧な動き。リズムの一体感。止めように
も止まらない感覚（？？？）。自信。威厳のようなもの。

　　　　めらめらともえる炎の
　　　　のこり火の
　　　　いつまでも
　　　　胸に残る

Sanjukta Panigrahi

It was after I came to the United States, in 1997, the news arrived that Sanjukta Panigrahi had passed away. I did not investigate or ask around for more information. I knew that she was 52 years old and I heard from Kumkum ji that she had recently not been able to dance as much as she had wished or expected because of an illness. After one performance, she was apparently crying in the green room. I wondered if she'd had knee problems or surgery; whether she'd had breast cancer. There was no clear information at that time.

I thought back to the time that I had visited her house in Bhubaneswar.
    Guruji entered the house while calling out,
    "Sanju! Sanju!"
    I followed after Guruji. Sanjukta came walking into the room in a gray, thin transparent saree hanging from her both shoulders. She didn't show much expression on her face and yet, she looked majestic.

She didn't speak a single word. I felt a little intimidated by her, feeling that maybe she was too majestic for me talk to.

I heard that Sanjukta used to meditate quietly for half an hour before a performance. This was after getting ready with all the costume and make up.

She did not tell anyone about her illness. Kumkum ji said that no one knew. I couldn't help thinking if everyone knew it and she accepted the encouragement from people around her, things may have been different...

She was Guruji's eminent disciple who made Odissi known in the world.

She was a person who changed my life completely. From the day I saw her dance at the Sogetsu Hall in 1983, I devoted my soul to dance.

Sanjukta lived such a short time and dedicated her life to dance.

左：カリフォルニア州オークランド、アメリカでの最後のコンサート
Left: Asako's last concert in Oakland California, U.S.A. 1/8/2005.

下：サンジュクタ パニグラヒの東京コンサートのチラシ（著者所有）
Below: The flyer of Sanjukta Panigrahi's concert in Tokyo, 1983.

Kumkum ji was also surprised by her premature death. She had not told anyone about her illness, until just before she passed away. I heard that it was breast cancer that had moved to her bone. For Sanjukta, there must have been a great struggle, but maybe she felt that there was no need to stay in the body that would not allow her to dance any more. I feel that she had moved far away from her body without hesitation.

How many people over the world had been impacted and touched by her dance? How many people felt that their souls were open because of her? I was certainly one of them. I saw the "Divine" clearly in her dance at the Sogetsu Hall in 1983. And my life changed completely. I did not understand completely at that time. She was partly in her body and partly not. It seemed as if she was present as herself but at the same time, she transcended herself. I felt there was a golden, brilliant light emanating from her whole body. The rhythm and the body were perfectly together. There was perfect movement. There was a unity of rhythm. No one could stop her dance. She had a certain confidence and a certain dignity.

the blazing flame
embers fire
remain in my heart
forever and ever

Photographed by Bob Giles

グル

　またデリーでの日々を思い出している。

　稽古場のお掃除のこと——。

　デリーのクムクムさんの家では、毎朝、踊りのクラスの前に、部屋の掃除をした。毎朝、クムクムさんから一対一で踊りを習っていたときのこと。クムクムさんのリビングルームが私たちの教室だった。練習用サリーに着替えたのち、クラスが始まる前に、最初にすることが掃除だった。まずインドのほうきで掃いて、水で濡らした布で拭く。それは毎朝のクラスの始まりのようなものだった。私が掃除をしていると、住み込みの、台所や掃除を手伝う若いネパール人の少年が、自分がやりたいと言った。彼はいつもやりたがった。掃除は彼の仕事だったから。でも、私は自分でしたかった。なぜかというと、掃除をすることは、自分にとって良いことをなのだとわかっていたから。稽古場を掃除して清めることは、踊りのためになる。ぜったいそうだ。だから踊りを教えてもらう前にまず、その場をきれいにすることが、私にとってとても大切だった。そうすることによって、よりよく学べる、あるいはより多く学べるような気がしたからだ。

リビングルームがきれいになると、クムクムさんのベッドルームから、ドゥーパのいい香りと煙がただよってきた。クムクムさんがプージャを終えて出てくる。ドゥーパとはお香ではなくて、黒い油のようなものだ。お香の一種で、黒っぽいものを燃やす。そして、部屋から出て来るクムクムさんはほんとうにきれいだった。新鮮な様子で美しかった。クムクムさんは私にプラサード（プージャのあとに下げてくるお供え物）を手渡す。それはだいたいいつも、彼女の庭にあるトゥルシ（ホーリーバジル）の葉。クムクムさんはアパートのテラスに、たくさんの美しい植物を育てていた。

　何度目かインドを訪れてからのことだった、ある時、クムクムさんは私からはもういっさいのお金を受け取りたくないとおっしゃった。私は彼女の家に泊まり、クムクムさんが料理を作って、私の面倒をみていた、私はクムクムさんの家族と同じものを食べていた。そう言われて、もうなんといったらいいのか、とまどってしまった。

　それよりもずっと前、日本にクムクムさんがいた頃は、生徒たちがお金を集め、感謝の気持ちとともにお渡ししていた。初めてインドに行ったときも、すこしばかりのお金をおいてきた。

でも、クムクムさんが私からお金を受け取らないと決めたときから、だんだんこう思うようになった。
　「クムクムさんのために何かできることはないかしら？」
　「教えてくださることに、感謝の気持ちを表わすにはどうしたら一番いいかしら？」
　私はいつもいつも、クムクムさんを幸せな気持ちにするにはいったいどうしたらいいかと考えるようになっていた。

　「ああ、私はこれが好きです」とクムクムさんが言ったり、夫のアショカさんがある店のナッツが好物と聞くと、ふたりが好きと言っているものをぜひとも手に入れようと思った。
　「私はあの花が好きです、その匂いが大好きです。」
　とクムクムさんが言えば、じゃ、次に行ったときには、それを買ってこようと思った。いつもいつも、クムクムさんが欲しがっているものはなんだろうと考えていた。何をお好きなのだろう？　どうすればご夫婦を幸せな気分にすることができるだろうか？　私が滞在している間、少しでも喜んでいただくにはどうすればいいんだろう？

　それは本当に、なんと言ったらいいのだろう。クムクムさんとの間柄が特別なものになっていったのだ。はっきりとそれまでとは違っていた。

クムクムさんが、例えば、この香りが好きです、とおっしゃると、どこ
に行けば最高のものが手にはいるだろうと考え始める。ときには、ブリ
ンダバンまで足をのばしたりする。

　まるでクリシュナ神の物語のようだった。まだクリシュナ神が若い頃、
牛飼い女のゴーピーたちと一晩中森で踊っていた。私はやっとそこにた
どり着いたような気持ちだった。いろいろな所に行って、お二人が喜び
そうなものを探す。そういうことは、すごく楽しかった。だけど、いつ
もいつも、まだ足りないと感じていた。だから、いつももっと他のもの
はないかと探していた。

　それから、クムクムさんは私にはあまりお金を使ってほしくないとも
思っていた。だから、手伝えることを見つけて、いつも楽しみながらし
ていた。私の使っていた部屋はアイロン部屋でもあったので、アイロン
かけが必要なもの全部がそこにあった。サリーのブラウスやらサリーや
ら。外にアイロンかけ専門の人がいて、本当に手早くサリーにアイロン
をかけていたので、だから、私は、時々クムクムさんのブラウスにアイ
ロンをかけた。ペチコートに穴が空いているのをみつけたら、繕ってあ
げたらいいなと思ってそうした。繕い物のほかに、作り物もした。ある
とき、カーテンを作ってくださいませんかと、クムクムさんに頼まれた

150

クムクムジー 日本で
Kumkum Laal in Japan.
Photographed by Ryosen Kono

ので、カーテンを作った。

　本当に、こんな気持ちになった相手はそう多くない。とても自然にこういうふうな気持ちが芽生えてきたのだ。クムクムさんが私が何かをやって、そのことに満足しているのを見ると、もうそれがこの世の最良のことだった。私はとっても幸せだった。何年もの間、振り返ってみると、インドで勉強している間ずっと、クムクムさんはとても丁寧に接してくれた。いつも私を、対等に扱ってくれた。踊りの教え以外は。教えてくれる時は、非常に厳しかったけど、でもそれは心を閉ざしたものではなくて、非常に気遣ってくれた上での厳しさだ。時には友だち同士のようで、時には姉妹のようだった。クムクムさんは最初から言っていた、
　「私はあなたがたの先生ではありません。私のことを姉のように考えてください。」
　クムクムさんは生徒たちと、そんなような関係を持ちたいと思っていたのだと思う。だから、いろいろなこと、個人的なこともたくさん話した。本当に親しくさせていただいた。

Guru

A few days ago, I got to thinking about Delhi again. In Kumkum ji's house, every morning, before we started class, I cleaned the dance room. I was taking private classes from Kumkum ji, every morning. We used her living room and it became our dance classroom. After changing my clothes and putting on a practice saree, right before the start of class, I would sweep with an Indian broom and mop with water and a cloth. While I was cleaning the room, the servant, the young Nepalese boy living there to help with the cooking and cleaning, also wanted to clean. When he saw me cleaning, he wanted to do it, because he felt that that was his work. However, I preferred to do it by myself and I knew it was something important for me. Learning dance would happen in a better way if I cleaned the dance floor, I felt.

When the living room was clean, the nice smell of dhoop and the smoke came from Kumkum ji's bedroom. She would finish her puja.

The dhoop is an incense used for the puja. She came out from the room looking beautiful and fresh. She gave me some prasad (food offerings taken from the alter after puja). It was usually some tulsi leaves from her garden outside. Although she was living in an apartment building, she still had beautiful plants on her balcony.

After I had been going to India a few times, she told me that she didn't want to take any money from me anymore. I was staying at her house. She was cooking; taking care of me and I was eating everything just like a member of her family. So I didn't know what to do.

In Japan as students, we had collected money and given her to thank her. When I went to India for the first time, I left some money to thank her.

But when she refused any money from me, it made me start thinking,
   "What can I do for her?"
   "What is the best way to say thank you for her teaching?"
   This made me think about her wishes all the time.

Sometimes she would say that she liked this or her husband Ashok ji liked a certain kind of nut from a certain shop. Then I would just go out and get that item. Kumkum ji said, "I like that flower, I love that smell."

I would automatically think that I could get that, next time. I was always trying to think what she or her husband may like.

In some ways this helped to develop a relationship with my teacher. It felt different from before. It was a little like Lord Krishna's story. When he was young, he was dancing all night with gopis in the forest. I felt I finally reached where he was. This situation made me go to different places to find something that would please them. That was also really fun. Yet a part of me always felt that I was not doing enough. I was always looking for something more to do for them.

Kumkum ji didn't want me to spend money on them. So I also enjoyed doing little jobs. My room was used as the ironing room, too. All the stuff to iron was there for instance the saree blouses and her sarees. The ironing person was outside and he provided a service, quickly ironing sarees. Sometimes I liked to iron her blouses. When her petticoat had a hole, I would think that maybe I could repair it. Along with mending things, I also made things. Kumkum ji once asked me to make curtains for that room.

The affection that I felt towards Kumkum ji, I didn't feel towards many people. It just came very naturally for her. When she was happy with something I had done, that was the best feeling. It made me happy. Looking back over the years, while I was there studying in India, Kumkum ji was very polite. She always treated me as her equal. When she was teaching, she was very strict but in a heartfelt way. She was very caring. Sometimes we were like friends and sometimes we were like sisters. She said from the beginning, "I'm not your teacher. You can think of me as an older sister."

She wanted to have that kind of relationship with her students. We would talk about different issues, sometimes personal topics. I am very grateful that I was able to have such a close relationship with her.

吉祥寺アムリタにて、日本での最後のコンサート
Her last concert in Japan at Kichijoji Amrita, Tokyo, 8/28/2005.
Photographed by Ryosen Kono

あとがき

　この本は、2004年の春から2006年まで、踊りを踊れなくなった期間に、ベッドの上で、踊りのこと、踊りの先生の思い出を一人考えたり想い起こしたりしつつ、なつかしみふりかえったものと、2007年の春から夏にかけてまとめたものである。2007年の秋にはクムクムジーが初渡米し、各都市でワークショップを行った。私は何年かぶりに師と出会い、師の踊りを見、その深さと美しさに再び踊ることに命が芽生えた。

　思えばずっと踊りに出会ってから、それなりの人生の変化転機の中にあり、いろいろな土地にありながら私は踊りから離れずにきたように思う。自分でもなんかびっくりしてしまう。踊りが私から離れなかったのは、私の出会った師が、師の教えが私の魂の深いところ、他の何もふれることがなかった、私の魂の奥深くに踊りを植えつけて下さったためだとつくづく思う。

この踊りにひかれる人々
なにかしらこれを読んだ方がたの
礎になればと思います。
　　　高見麻子

　（高見麻子さんは2007年11月3日に永眠されました。師クムクム
ラール氏は同年10月に来米、二人はいっしょに過ごすことができまし
た。この「あとがき」はクムクム氏がインドへの帰途に着いたあと、お
そらく、麻子さんご本人が旅立つ直前に書かれました。／編者註）

Afterword

I wrote this book, from 2004 to 2006. I was no longer able to dance back then. It is a collection of my thoughts about the dance and the memories of the dance teachers that I recollected enjoying. I was missing those days, while on my bed. Also some pieces were written in the spring to summer of 2007. In the autumn of 2007, Kumkum ji came to the U.S. for the first time, and held some workshops in several cities. I was reunited with my guru for the first time in years, and I saw her dance again. Her dance inspired me with its depth and beauty. It ignited my desire to dance again.

Since I discovered this dance a long time ago, I have had some turning points in my life and lived in many different places. All this time, I have never ever left dance. It amazes me. I believe that, because my guru's teaching reached the deepest place in my soul, a place no one had touched, the dance did not leave me. My guru kindly planted the dance seed in my deepest soul. That made the dance stay with me.

To people who are drawn by this dance,
Those who read this,
I hope to become their foundation for something.
Asako Takami

(Asako Takami went to sleep on November 3rd, 2007. Kumkum Laal had come to the United States in October of that same year and both of them were able to spend time together. This "afterword" was written when Kumkum ji was on her way back home to India. This "afterword" must have been written just before Asako herself took off. / Editor)

麻子とコンテンポラリーダンス

ラルフ レモン

　麻子がオディッシーを踊っている姿を見ると、僕はいつも泣いてし
まった。

　ふたりで踊りを創ったとき、彼女はたいへんオープンだった。とにか
くなんでもやってみようとしていた。そして、それは時間のかかること
でもあった。(チベット仏教の)多羅菩薩のような静かなる激しさでもっ
て動いているときでさえも、彼女の動きには崇高とも言える本質的な静
けさがあった。

　初めていっしょに創る作業を始めたとき、どの曲だったのか覚えてい
ないが、彼女がオディッシーを踊る、その側で僕は即興的に踊ってみた。
彼女は僕のことを気に留めていないようだった。僕の存在は彼女の邪魔
ではなかったし、僕は創造的に邪魔にならないようにしようとしていた。
麻子は自分の領域に立って（踊って）いた。彼女の踊りのスピリットは、
豊かな空間を周囲に持っていた。なんとなんと優しい空間だろう。

2回目には、僕は彼女に即興的に踊ってみてはどうだろうと頼んだ。僕のモダンダンスのグループといっしょに。ダンサーたちの中で、彼女は凍りついたように立ちすくんでいた。じっと静止したままで、周りで起きていること全部を見ていた。僕たちは彼女のまわりで踊った。彼女の知らない、見たこともない踊りの言語で。ほとんど20分ほどになるか、彼女はじっと止まったままだった。目を大きく見開き、あらゆる情報をできるかぎり取り入れていた。取り入れたものを噛み砕くために、その時間を使っていたのだ。スタジオでのあの日以来、彼女はあらゆることを試してみた。毎日、ふたりの作業は進み育っていった。そしてそれは「Tree」（2000年）という劇場で発表する、一公演分の長さの作品に発展していった。彼女の恐れを知らない（そしてしなやかな）包容力のある体は、異国情緒あふれ、確固たる、そして根源的に必要とされるなにかを付け加えながら、動いた。僕のモダンダンス実験にとっては非常に特別な感じで。

　麻子はまた、すばらしい表現者だった。彼女のパフォーマンス——その時間、そのエネルギー、その空間。僕がいっしょに創造したダンサーの中には、彼女のようなパフォーマンスができるものはほとんどいない。麻子はダンスの天才だと思う。

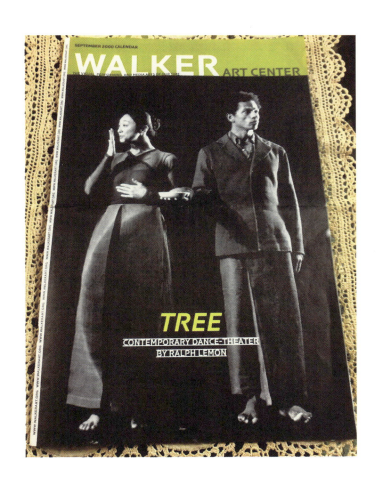

(ラルフ レモン：振り付け師、モダンダンサー、コンセプテュアリズム アーティスト。2015年、前米国大統領オバマ氏から National Medal of Arts を受賞。ラルフと麻子は、コンテンポラリーダンス作品「Tree」を 2000 年に発表した。)

Asako and contemporary dance

Ralph Lemon

I cried every time I saw her dance Odissi.

Asako was exceptionally open in our work together. Would try anything. But would take her time. Her time was evanescent. She had a sublime constitutional stillness, even when moving with all her Tara-like quiet fierceness.

When we first began working together I danced, improvised along side an Odissi dance she shared (I can't remember which one). She didn't seem bothered; I was not a distraction, which is what I was creatively attempting. She stood (danced) her ground. Her dancing sprit had such a generous space around it.

The second time we worked together I asked her to improvise, with my group of modern dancers. She stood frozen within the group. Stock-still, watching all that was going on. We danced around her in a movement language she didn't know, had never seen, for a good twenty minutes and she never moved. She was using that

168

作品「Tree」マヌランジャン プラダンと。
"Tree" with Sri Manoranjan Pradhan.
Photographed by T Charles Erickson

time, eyes wide open, to take in the information, as best she could, her translation. After that day in the studio she tried everything, everyday as our work together grew and became an evening length theater-dance work titled, Tree (2000). Her fearless (and gentle) capacious body moved in a way that was quite special for my modern dance experiments, adding something foreign and emphatic and ultimately necessary.

Asako was also a remarkable performer. Could hold a performance, time, energy and space like few dancers I've ever worked with. I think Asako was a dance genius.

(Ralph Lemon is a choreographer, modern dancer, and conceptualism artist. He received the National Medal of Arts from the former President of the United States of America Mr. Obama in 2015. He and Asako together created a contemporary dance presentation Tree in 2000.)

From her journal／日記より

October 12 2004

When I woke up the inside of my mouth and tongue were not feeling good.

I did qigong massage and after that did breathing,

focusing on not pushing my breath much.

Breathing gently, softly and cleansing.

Picturing Guruji's golden body and Kumkumji's fragrance.

October 13 2004

Inside my body feels light. Breath comes in deep.

Lots of space inside my body, to find something fresh from meditation.

Today started with a rabbit and ended with a frog.

A frog can survive in the desert.

I didn't know that.

October 14 2004

Frog walks across my meditation again.

And he showed me he was not a frog.

Wind was blowing and cold. I changed places.

And then went back home.

My body was cold inside and I couldn't fix it.

October 15 2004

Warm and spacious inside my body.

And comfortable with that space being still there.

I wanted to sit more but started my day.

October 18 2004

Watching my breath.

Inside my body my organs are soft and warm.

Concentrating on effort.

Mindfully accomplish the work.

Still failing to control my craving for sweets.

(from random notes)

lots of dancing

doesn't mean

from deep. go deep. and not just moving your arms and feels

meaninglessly.

You are in deep meditation.

It has to come from your daily practice, from deep mediation.

The place when you are in and from there, find "the wilderness"

（原文は英語／編者註）

　私は、踊っている人の目が、味・色・においを帯びるとき、そこにラサを感じます。

謝辞

　以下のみなさまの惜しみない協力のおかげで、この本を形にすることができました。本当にありがとうございました。（アルファベット順）

　Sri Vishnu Tattva Das 特にオディッシーの歴史についてアドバイスをいただきました。

　Bob Giles 素晴らしいポートレート写真を提供してくださいました。

　Andreana Karabotsios「グル」の章を聞き取り、文字に起こしてくださいました。Bessie、Chaitee ともに麻子さんのアメリカでのダンス活動を支えました。

　河野亮仙さん 貴重で詳細な資料と日本での美しい舞台写真を提供してくださいました。麻子さんの日本での活動をさまざまな形で支援されました。

　Ralph Lemon コンテンポラリーダンスについて寄稿してくださいました。

　Vasanta Rao 英訳の校正のほかに、さまざまな私の質問にていねいに答えてくださいました。

　佐瀬絹子さん 心よく出版を許し、大切な家族写真を提供してくださいました。

　Chaitee Sengupta 写真を提供してくださいました。麻子さんのドラムは彼女のもとで大切に保管されています。

Acknowledgments

I would like to thank the people who contributed their time and work for this book. Without their support, this book could not have been born.

I thank, in alphabetical order,

Sri Vishnu Tattva Das: He gave me advice, especially on the history of Odissi.

Bob Giles: His beautiful portrait photos adorn this book.

Andreana Karabotsios: Asako dictated the chapter "Guru" to her. Together with Chaitee and Bessie, she supported Asako's dance career in the U.S.

Ryosen Kono: He offered beautiful concert photos and detailed documentation, especially on Asako's career in Japan. He supported her in many ways, from her early time in Japan.

Ralph Lemon: He wrote about Asako's works in contemporary dance.

Vasanta Rao: She helped with proofreading/editing the English draft and also kindly answered many of my questions.

Chaitee Sengupta: She kindly shared some photos including Asako's pakhawaj drum which is with her.

Kinuko Sase: She kindly let me publish this book and offered some of the precious family photos from Asako's early life.

略歴

　1960年4月19日新潟市に生まれる。女子美術短期大学在学中にインド舞踊に出会う。茗荷谷・林泉寺で、康米那氏のレクチャーデモンストレーションに感動し、「かんみなタゴールダンスを踊る会」に通うようになる。マニプリ、カタカリの基礎、タゴールダンスを習う。1983年のサンジュクタ パニグラヒ氏の日本公演で魂を揺さぶられるような体験をする。直後、来日したクムクム ラール氏に出会い、オディッシーダンスに魅せられる。ラール氏のクラスは1日数時間、週に4日ほどの本格的なものだった。3年後にはパドマビブーシャン グル ケルチャラン モハパトラ氏が来日、2ヵ月に及ぶ集中レッスンの機会に恵まれる。マリニ スブラマニアン氏にインド古典歌唱の手ほどきも受けインド芸術に恋をする。

　インドに戻ったラール氏を追うように、1987年にインドに渡る。オリッサ州ブバネシュワールにその年開校したばかりのオディッシー リサーチ センターで、グル ケルチャラン モハパトラ、グル ガンガーダール プラダーン、グル ラマニ ランジャン ジェナの指導を受ける。さらに、パッカワージ（オディッシーの音楽を演奏する太鼓）をデリーでグル トリナート マハラナに、サンスクリット語を大西正幸博士に学ぶ。踊りに夢中で、周りの人の理解と支援に恵まれ何度もインドに行って勉強を続ける。

1990 年代に入ってからムクンド スブラマニアン氏（マリニ スブラマニア
ン氏の子息）とサンフランシスコへ居を移す。スブラマニアン氏の研究のた
めに青森県に長期滞在したりもする。1997 年頃、サンフランシスコに戻り踊
りを教え始める。パラヴィ ダンスグループと名付ける。日本では増上寺で始
まり、鎌倉・安養院、早稲田銅鑼魔館、上野護国寺・大黒天、五反田・本立寺、
延命寺、近江楽堂と各地で多くの公演活動をする。時には 1 日に 3 回も違う
場所で公演したこともあった。そして渡米後 7 年目には気がつくとアメリカ
中を旅して踊ってきたと記している。

　1999 年頃ラルフ レモン氏と出会いコンテンポラリーダンスを試みる。レモ
ン氏の振り付けで「Tree, Part 2 in Geography Trilogy」を発表（2000 年）。
その年サンフランシスコで、「イザドラ ダンカン ダンス賞個人パフォーマン
ス部門」の最終選考に残る。「The Piper」Yasmen Sorab Mehta（カリフォ
ルニア コンテンポラリー ダンサーズ）による振り付け。

　多くの友人の求めに応えて、2005 年 1 月 8 日オークランド友人宅でコンサ
ート。その夏の 8 月 28 日東京、吉祥寺で公演。最後の公演となった。

　2007 年 11 月 3 日旅立つ。サンフランシスコ、ゴールデンゲートパークの
静かな湖畔に眠る。

Profile

Born in Niigata-shi, Japan on April 19th, 1960. While studying at Joshibi University of Arts and Design, she first encountered with Indian dance in the school classroom. In the same year, inspired by Smt. Mina Kang's lecture demonstration at Myogadani Rinsenji temple, joined "Mina Kang Tagore Dance Club". Learned Manipuri, Kathakali basics, and Tagore dance. Smt. Sanjukta Panigrahi's concert in Tokyo in 1983 deeply touched her soul. Soon after that, met with Smt. Kumkum Laal who lived in Tokyo. The class was offered long hours all day on somewhat like 4 days a week. Asako was fascinated by Odissi dance. 3 years later, had an opportunity to join the 2 months intensive workshop by Padma Vibhushan Guru Kelucharan Mohapatra. Also studied Indian Classical vocal under Smt. Malini Subramanian. Asako fell in love with Indian arts.

Following Smt. Kumkum Laal who moved to India in 1987, Asako studied in India under Guru Kelucharan Mohapatra, Guru Gangadhar Pradhan, and Guru Ramani Ranjan Jena at Odissi Research Center which opened that year. In addition, she studied Packhawaj (the drum that accompanies Odissi dance) with Guru Trinath Maharana in Delhi; and Sanskrit with Dr. Masayuki Ohnishi. With support and understanding from the people around her, she continued to visit India for training.

In 1990's, she moved to San Francisco with Mukund Subramanian (the son of Smt. Malini Subramanian). Stayed in Aomori, Japan for

Mukund's extensive research for a few years. When she returned to San Francisco around 1997, she started teaching dance. She named her community Pallavi Dance Group. Started at Zojoji temple, she gave many performances in Japan such as Anyoin Kamakura, Waseda Doramakan, Ueno Gokokuji Daikokuten temple, Honryuji temple in Gotanda, Enmeiji in Urawa, Konoe Gakudo, etc. On some occasions, she performed 3 times at different places on a day. She wrote that after living in the U.S. for 7 years, she had traveled all over the continent to dance.

Asako also explored contemporary dance with Ralph Lemon who she met around 1999. She performed in Tree, Part 2 in Geography Trilogy, choreographed by Ralph Lemon (2000). She was nominated by the Isadora Duncan Awards Committee as a finalist for the best performance in Individual performance division for The Piper, choreographed by Yasmen Sorab Mehta, California Contemporary Dancers.

She performed at the private resident in Oakland, California in front of her good friends on January 8, 2005. In the same year, performed at Kichijoji in Tokyo on August 28, 2005. This was her last concert.

Dparted on November 3, 2007. Rest in peace by the pond in San Francisco Golden Gate Park.

日本での主な活動

河野亮仙まとめ

タゴールダンス時代

1980年5月 四谷公会堂 ダゴール祭ダンスドラマ「チットラゴダ」主人公チットラゴダ王女の友人役で出演

1980年12月、1981年12月、1983年1月 林泉寺にて発表会

1983年5月 中野文化センター タゴール祭「バーヌシンホポダポリ」クリシュナ役

オディッシー時代

1984年10月21日 増上寺ホールにて インド祭りの音楽舞踊祭

1985年5月 渋谷「タゴール歌曲の夕べ」松田美沙さんとオディッシーの振り付けで、タゴールの曲を上演

1985年10月「ラーマヤーナ」ダンスパート

1988年 青山円形劇場 AKI STUDIO (ジャズダンス公演)タンジェリンドリームの曲に振り付けて

1988年6月28日 鎌倉安養院にて「吉田麻子 GITA GOVINDA を踊る」インド絵画研究会主催

1989年3月18日 赤坂ウイナーズにて インド絵画研究会/赤坂トレビ主催

1989年4月1日 有楽町西武6階 ファブリックギャラリーにて展示会イベント 赤坂トレビ主催

1989年10月4日 TBS ホールにて「インドの夕べ」（井上貴子、佐倉永治、吉田麻子）

1989年11月10、18日 早稲田銅羅魔館にて 早稲田銅羅魔館 主催

1990年6月7、8日 赤坂駐車場特設ステージにて「赤さか丸ごとライブ90」赤坂トレビ主催

1990年10月10日 五反田本立寺にて「チララ祭」チララの絆を救う会主催

1991年5月3日 奥久慈 水府村にて「インド古典舞踊公演」水府村主催

1991年5月18日 世田谷区の善養寺大法会にて

1991年 チララの絆を救う会関連で、アンドラプラデッシュ州チララへ

1991年8月8日 かわさき IBM ギャラリーにて「伊藤恭介／河野亮仙写真展」レセプション

1997年6月11日 赤坂コミュニティぷらざにて「インド古典舞踊の夕べ」久保田幸代さんと

1997年10月4日 すみだリバーサイドホールにて「インド舞踊祭」（ナマステインディア関連イベント）

1997年10月10日 上野公園 護国寺大黒天にて「奉納インド古典舞踊と音楽」

1999年10月30日 JML セミナー レクチャーデモンストレーション JML 主催

1999年11月6日 浦和 延命寺にて「サンフランシスコのインド舞踊」

2005年8月28日 吉祥寺スタジオ アムリタにて「アジアン特急」ミーナさんと はるばる屋主催

Works in Japan

compiled by Ryosen Kono

Tagore Dance

May, 1980 Played the friend of the princess Chitrangada in Dance drama "Chitrangada" for Tagore Festival at Yotsuya Kokaido.

December of1980, December of 1981, January of 1983 Students recitals at Rinsen-ji temple.

May, 1983 Played Lord Krishna roll in "Bhanu Singher Podaboli" for Tagore Festival at Nakano Culture Center.

Odissi Dance

October 21, 1984 Indian festival at Zojoji temple hall.

May, 1985 "A night of songs from Tagore" Performed Tagore's song in Odissi choreography with Misa Matsuda.

October, 1985 "Ramayana" dancing part

1988, AKI STUDIO (Jazz dance) recital at Aoyama Enkei Gekijo. Choreographed "Tangerine Dream."

June 28, 1988 "Asako Yoshida dances Gita Govinda" at Kamakura Anyoin temple, organized by Indian Painting Study Group.

March 18, 1989 Performed at Akasaka Winners organized by Indian Painting Study Group/Akasaka Trevi.

April 1, 1989 Performed at Yurakucho Seibu Fablic Gallery organized by Akasaka Trevi.

October 4, 1989 "A night of India" at TBS Hall (Takako Inoue, Eiji Sakura, Asako Yoshida)

November 10, 18, 1989 Performed at Waseda Drama Kan organized by Waseda Drama Kan.

June 7, 8, 1990 "Akasaka Marugoto Live 90", organized by Akasaka Trevi.

October 10,1990 "Chirala Festival" at Honryuji temple in Gotanda organized by Chirala handloom weaving conservation group.

May 3, 1991 "Indian Classical Dance concert" at Okukuji organized by Suihu-mura

May 18, 1991 Performed at Daiho-e at Zenyouji temple in Setagaya

1991 Visited Chirala, Andhra Pradesh state, India organized by Chirala handloom weaving conservation group

August 8, 1991 Performed at Kyosuke Itoh/Ryosen Kono photo exhibit recaption at Kawasaki IBM Gallery

June 11, 1997 "A Night of Indian Classical Dance" with Sachiyo Kubota

October 4, 1997 "Indian Dance Festival" ("Namaste India" events related) at Sumida Riverside Hall

October 10, 1997 "Indian Classical Dance and Music Offering" at Gokokuji temple Daikokuten in Ueno Park

October 30, 1999 Lecture demonstration at JML Seminar organized by JML

November 6, 1999 "Indian Dance in San Francisco" at Enmeiji temple, Urawa

August 28, 2005 "Asian Express" with Meena organized by Harubaruya

あとがきのあとがき

　高見麻子さんに出会ったのは2004年の夏、私がカリフォルニア州に移住してすぐの頃だった。カリフォルニア大学のあるバークレーという街で、煉瓦作りの大きな、昔は倉庫だったような建物の中にあるダンススタジオでオディッシーのクラスを教えていた。インド古典舞踊に惹かれていた私は、片道1時間車を走らせて習いに行ったのだ。そこは、大きな天井の高い建物で、中はいくつもの部屋に分かれていて、ダンスを練習する部屋がいくつかと、そのほかには、天井からなにやら器具がぶらさがっているサーカスの曲芸のようなことを練習できる部屋や、ガラス工房やらが混在していて、芸術を篤く支援している街の姿勢が感じられるような場所。麻子さんが、ステップを小気味よく踏むと、とてもいい音が部屋にひろがった。オディッシーの基本のひとつに、何十とある手の型（ムドラー）を覚えるが、麻子さんが一つ一つの手の型を示しながら、ムドラーの名前をつぎつぎに唱えると、もうそれは妙なる音楽になっていて、起承転結がある一曲の踊りのようで、私は不思議な気持ちになったものだった。麻子さんは存在すべてが、踊りであり、音楽であり、美であった。

その頃は、最初の手術の後で、麻子さんはすでにガンの闘病をされていた。すぐに仲良くなり、ふたりでこの本を作ろうと話した。一番最初に書いたのが、「クムクムさんのクムクム」。私は、その後、クムクム ラール先生に初めてお会いしたとき、一番楽しみだったことの一つが、先生の額の「ほんもののビンディー」をこの目で確かめることだった。その数年後、オイルで赤いクムクムの粉を丸く額につけている方にもうひとり、お会いした。代表的なオディッシーの踊り手のひとりであるイリアナ チトラスチさんだ。

　この本の文章は麻子さんの手書きの原稿のほかに、手紙であったり、メールであったり、コンピュータの中に発見された未発表の文であったり、聞き取って文字に起こしたものであったりする。なるべく、原文をそのまま載せるように努めたが、一部、編者が補ってあるところもある。事象の間違えがあるかもしれないことを許してほしい。もっともっと書いてもらいたかったのだが、運命がそうさせなかった。そのかわりのように、ボブ ギレスさんと河野亮仙さんの美しい写真が集まってきた。イラストレーションはすべて麻子さんの作品だ。

　クムクム先生は2007年10月20日に、サンフランシスコでソロコンサートを上演された。その会場に、麻子さんは車椅子でかけつけた。公

の場に姿を見せたのはそれが最後になったと思う。クムクム先生は涙を流して、麻子さんがご病気でとても胸を痛めていると舞台で話された。その時、踊ったのは、「ナマミ マンガラチャラン」、「アーラビ パーラヴィ」、「ヤミ ヘ」、「モクシャ」。モクシャが終わると、会場にいた人々は、普段のコンサートなら出演したアーティストつまりクムクム先生の元にかけつけるだろうが、その時はみんなが麻子さんのところにかけつけた。後で、クムクム先生と私はそのことを話してはくすっと笑った。

　そのコンサートのすぐ後に、ニハリカ モハンティさんの呼びかけで麻子さんの医療費の助けになるようにチャリティ コンサートを開催した。サンフランシスコ ベイエリアのダンサーたちが集まった。もちろんクムクム先生も踊った。クムクム先生は黄色いサリーで、
　「これは麻子からもらったサリーです」
とおっしゃった。

　前の日、クムクム先生から習ったばかりの「シュリ ラーマ」を練習するために、バークレーで私たち初心者組は集まった。練習の帰り、偶然、バークレーに泊まっていたクムクム先生を私は当時まだ赤ちゃんだった息子といっしょに車に乗せ、サンフランシスコの麻子さんの家にお連れした。ひさしぶりに麻子さんに会えた。神様の采配だった。麻子さんの

献身的なパートナーだったラルフ レモンさんは、クムクム先生がアパートに着くと所用で出かけてしまった。クムクム先生と麻子さんと息子と静かな美しい秋の陽のさす午後だった。麻子さんは日本語で、

「クムクムさん、もうすぐ発つのですね。なんてこと。明日のコンサートの準備はここでして——」

と話しかけていた。息子は眠ってしまい、麻子さんもときどきうつらうつらと眠りに落ちる。クムクム先生は、祭壇に向かって座ると、

「話をしてもいいですよ」

と私たちにおっしゃった。そうして数珠を手にお祈りを始めた。今でもそのときのことを思い出すと涙が止まらない。クムクム先生の清らかな存在が部屋を満たした。帰る時間がきて、私は麻子さんとじっくりと抱擁をして、最後のお別れをした。麻子さんは

「きっと治るって信じてるから」

とおっしゃった。涙があふれて何も言えなかったけど、私はなんどもなんども首をたてにふった。そのときのことを私はクムクム先生にとても感謝している。そして麻子さんにも。

麻子さんが亡くなった後、奇跡のように私たちは大きな家族になった。彼女を愛していた友だちがみんな家族のように親しくなったのだ。誰もが麻子さんを心から好きだったから。

ここ数年、昔、麻子さんと親しかった、いっしょによく練習されていたヴィシュヌー タッタヴァ ダス先生に踊りを習うようになった。初めてヴィシュヌー先生のワークショップに参加した日のことは忘れられない。ヴィシュヌー先生が生徒たちの前で踊っていると突然、部屋が暖かいエネルギーで満ち溢れてくるのだ。驚いた。ああこれは、麻子さんが踊っていたときも同じだったなあ。なんと懐かしい。私の中の奥の方にずっと昔に閉じてしまったものが、開いた。息を吹き返した。同じことを、麻子さんはクムクム先生のクラスで体験されたと書いている。オディッシーという踊りにはこういう力がある。

　ふりかえると、麻子さんといっしょに過ごすことができたのは、とても短い間だった。出会って少ししたら、踊りを教えることができなくなってしまった。オークランドの自宅は引き払い、ニューヨークとサンフランシスコとアリゾナの仏教リトリートセンターとあちこちで療養されていた。

　でも亡くなってからあともずっと続けて、麻子さんは私にたくさんのことを教えてくださったんだとつくづく思う。踊りを練習していると、「ここをこうしてみたら？」と麻子さんの声が聞こえてくるようだ。こ

の本を出版することができて、心から感謝し、満足し、幸せに感じている。最後に、七月堂の知念明子さんと七月堂に導いてくださったタゴール歌唱の奥田由香さんに篤くお礼を申し上げたい。

2019 年 1 月 田中晴子

Afterword of afterword

Asako Takami and I met in 2004, soon after I moved to the San Francisco Bay area from Tokyo, Japan. She was teaching Odissi dance in Berkeley, California. The dance studio was in a big, old building made of adobe bricks, perhaps a former warehouse. I was drawn to learning Indian classical dance and went to learn from her despite the hour long drive. The building was divided into a few rooms with high ceilings. Some of the rooms were dance studios; one room was for practicing acrobatics; another room was a glass art studio. The building reflected the city's support for the arts.

When Asako danced, the sound of her feet stepping and stamping filled the room nicely. One of the fundamental techniques of Odissi dance is the use of hand gestures, called mudras. When Asako recited the names of the mudras and then demonstrated them one by one, it sounded like a piece of beautiful, meditative music. I felt as if it were a dance song with introduction, verse, and ending. I was mesmerized. Her whole being was the dance, the music, and the beauty.

When I first met Asako, it was after her first surgery. She was already fighting cancer. We had an immediate rapport and got along very well. We made a plan to create this book. The first piece she wrote in her memoir was, "Kumkum ji's kumkum." When I finally met Kumkum ji in person, one of the things I really looked forward to, was seeing the actual bindi or kumkum on her forehead. A few years after that, I met another person who painted a red bindi with oil and red powder. She was Smt. Ileana Citaristi, a well known exponent of Odissi dance.

This book is a collection of Asako's hand written pieces as well as her letters and emails to me. Some compositions were on her computer, and also included is an interview by Andreana Karabotsios. I've tried my best to keep her original work, however, there are some places I edited a little. I take responsibility for any mistakes and I ask the kind readers' forgiveness for any such mistakes. I wished that Asako could have written more but her situation didn't allow it. Instead, Bob Giles and Ryosen Kono generously shared with me their beautiful photographs. All the paintings and drawings are Asako's own art.

Kumkum ji visited San Francisco and presented a solo concert on October 20th, 2007. Asako came to the concert in a wheelchair. I think that was Asako's last public appearance. That day on stage, Kumkum ji spoke of her deep sorrow in seeing Asako's suffering from illness. She was in tears. Kumkum ji danced the following items, beautifully: Namami Mangalacharan, Arabi Pallavi, Yami He, and Moksha. Typically, with the completion of Moksha, the audience goes to the dancer and congratulates them. However, on this occasion, everybody stood up and went to see Asako. Later, Kumkum ji and I talked about this moment and laughed together.

Soon after that concert, Smt. Niharika Mohanty organized a fundraising concert to support Asako's medical expenses. Many of the classical dancers in the San Francisco Bay Area danced in the event. Kumkum ji also danced. She was in a yellow saree and announced, "Asako gave me this saree."

One day before the benefit concert, I went to meet with some of Asako's students to practice the item, Sri Rama, which we had just learned from Kumkum ji. Unexpectedly, it happened that I picked Kumkum ji up, in Berkeley, where she was staying and drove her to Asako's place in San Francisco. My baby son was with me at the time. I hadn't seen Asako for long time. God must have had a hand in this plan. I saw Asako in person for the last time that day. Her devoted partner, Ralph Lemon, left the house soon after we arrived to do some errands. It was such a quiet beautiful autumn afternoon. Asako was speaking to Kumkum ji in Japanese.

"Kumkum ji, you are leaving so soon. Oh, I can't believe it... Please get ready here at my place, for the performance tomorrow..."

My son was asleep. Asako also fell in and out of sleep.

Kumkum ji found a seat in front of the alter for herself and took out her rosary.

"You two can speak", she said. And she started praying. When I think about that day, I cannot hold back my tears. The room was filled with Kumkum ji's virtuous presence. When I finally had to leave, Asako and I hugged a long time to say good bye. She said,

"I still believe I will get well."

I couldn't say anything because of tears, but I nodded my head, yes, again and again.

I am grateful to Kumkum ji for that day. And also to Asako.

After Asako left, all of us became like a big family. Her friends who loved her became very close to each other. I believe that this is because everybody was so fond of her.

I started learning Odissi dance from Sri Vishnu Tattva Das a few years ago. Vishnu ji was Asako's close friend and they used to dance together often. I cannot forget the first time that I joined his workshop. Vishnu ji was dancing in front of us. Suddenly I felt the room was filled with nice, warm energy. I was very surprised. This was the same feeling I had when Asako was dancing. Something deep inside of me which was closed up and forgotten for a long time after Asako's departure, started breathing again. How sweet it was! Asako wrote that she experienced the same thing in Kumkum ji's class. Odissi dance has such a beautiful quality, that can make these experiences possible.

When I look back, I realize that Asako and I spent only a short time together. Soon after I joined her class, she wasn't able to teach dance that much. She packed up her place in Oakland and moved to New York. She spent some time in New York, some time in San Francisco, and some in the Buddhist retreat center in Arizona.

However, I truly feel that she taught me so many things even after she passed away. Whenever I am rehearsing dance, I can hear her voice something like this:

"Would you do this in this way?"

I am deeply thankful to Akiko Chinen of Shichigatsu-do for being able to publish this book and to Tagore singer, Yuka Okuda who connected me to Shichigatsu-do. With appreciation and contentment, I am very much in happiness.

January, 2019

Haruko Tanaka

本書はクラウドファンディングを通して多くのご支援をいただいて制作されました。感謝の意をこめて支援者のお名前をここに掲載いたします。またお名前の掲載を辞退された方、さまざまな形で支援してくださった方が大勢いらっしゃいましたことをここに記します。

The creation of this book was made possible with the support of many people through the crowdfunding campaign. I deeply appreciate the generosity of the supporters.
In addition, there are many people who helped with the production but prefer to remain anonymous. I am grateful to all. Thank you.

Pulkit Desai

Yuko Gower

Shinobu Hataji

Fumihiko Higashijo

Saori Homfray

Mariko Komae

Mythili Kumar

Ralph Lemon

Niharika Mohanty

Ayano Nagaoka

Yuki Nara

Satoko Ogawa

Yuka Okuda

Toshihide Tanaka

成田長仁

佐藤秀平

佐藤京子

著者	高見麻子
イラスト	高見麻子
書き起こし／翻訳／編集	田中晴子
英文校正	ヴァサンタ ラオ
写真	ボブ ギレス
	河野亮仙
	T チャールス エリクソン
	佐瀬絹子
	チャイティ セングプタ
協力	河野亮仙
	ラルフ レモン
	ヴィシュヌー タッタヴァ ダス

Author	Asako Takami
Illustrations	Asako Takami
Editor	Haruko Tanaka
English proofreading and editing	Vasanta Rao
Photographs	Bob Giles
	Ryosen Kono
	T Charles Erickson
	Kinuko Sase
	Chaitee Sengupta
Contribution	Ryosen Kono
	Ralph Lemon
	Vishnu Tattva Das

インド回想記　オディッシーダンサー 高見麻子

2019年4月19日　発行

著　者　高見　麻子
発行者　知念　明子
発行所　七　月　堂
　　　〒156-0034　東京都世田谷区松原2-26-6
　　　電話 03-3325-5717　FAX 03-3325-5731

印刷・製本：渋谷文泉閣

©2019 Asako Takami
Printed in Japan　ISBN 978-4-87944-369-4　C0095
乱丁本・落丁本はお取り替えいたします。